T0209146

COMMITTED
DIFFICULT
PLACE

Being

in a

VERNADETTE R. AUGUSTUSEL

WESTBOW
PRESS®
A DIVISION OF THOMAS NELSON
& ZONDERVAN

This book is a work of non-fiction. Unless otherwise noted, the author
and the publisher make no explicit guarantees as to the accuracy of
the information contained in this book and in some cases, names of
people and places have been altered to protect their privacy.

WestBow Press books may be ordered through booksellers or by contacting:

WestBow Press
A Division of Thomas Nelson & Zondervan
1663 Liberty Drive
Bloomington, IN 47403
www.westbowpress.com
844-714-3454

Because of the dynamic nature of the Internet, any web addresses or
links contained in this book may have changed since publication and
may no longer be valid. The views expressed in this work are solely those
of the author and do not necessarily reflect the views of the publisher,
and the publisher hereby disclaims any responsibility for them.

Any people depicted in stock imagery provided by Getty Images are models,
and such images are being used for illustrative purposes only.
Certain stock imagery © Getty Images.

Unless otherwise noted, scripture quotations marked (NIV) are taken
from the Holy Bible, New International Version®, NIV®. Copyright
© 1973, 1978, 1984, 2011 by Biblica, Inc.™ Used by permission of
Zondervan. All rights reserved worldwide. www.zondervan.com The
"NIV" and "New International Version" are trademarks registered in
the United States Patent and Trademark Office by Biblica, Inc.™

Scripture quotations marked (AMP) are taken from the
Amplified Bible, Copyright © 1954, 1958, 1962, 1964, 1965,
1987 by The Lockman Foundation. Used by permission.

ISBN: 978-1-9736-9354-3 (sc)
ISBN: 978-1-9736-9353-6 (e)

Library of Congress Control Number: 2020910447

Print information available on the last page.

WestBow Press rev. date: 12/23/2020

Contents

Introduction

Being committed in a difficult place is a challenging choice we all will face at one point and time. In this life, we will be challenged in all types of situations and circumstances. There will be challenges in our relationships, careers, finances, and health. How we respond, act, react, and handle ourselves in difficult times is crucial, especially when making life-changing decisions and choices. The peace you should have during such times the world cannot give to you, and you can't allow anything or anyone to take it away. Jesus said, "Peace I leave with you; my peace I give you. I do not give to you as the world gives. Do not let your hearts be troubled and do not be afraid" (John 14:27).

There is going come a time when we will have to take a stance, a stand, a determination, and a decision that nothing shall move us from a peaceful state of being, and you are going to keep your peace regardless of what is going on. The peace that God gave and left with us is ours to keep. Don't be distracted, don't be derailed; stay focused. "Therefore, since we are surrounded by such a great cloud of witnesses, let us throw off everything that hinders and the sin that so easily entangles. And let us run with perseverance the race marked out for us, fixing our eyes on Jesus, the pioneer and perfecter of faith. For the joy set before him he endured the cross, scorning its shame, and sat down at the right hand of the throne of God" (Hebrews 12:1–2).

Your mindset shall not be persuaded to surrender your peace at any cost. We should be reminded of our brother Paul and how he responded during difficult times and what he stated in Philippians. Paul said in so many words that he had learned the art of being content. That is it; one of the things we need to learn is how to be content, no matter what. Paul then went on to say, "I am not saying this because I am in need, for I have learned to be content whatever the circumstances. I know what it is to be in need, and I know what it is to have plenty. I have learned the secret of being content in any and every situation, whether well fed or hungry, whether living in plenty or in want. I can do all this through him who gives me strength" (Philippians 4:11–13). So being content is not just about what you have or don't have. It is also about your mindset, and holding on to the peace of God, his power, and his presences, just to name a few. As we journey through this book, we will discover empowerment principles and spiritual discipline that will help us to stand and be committed in the difficult seasons of life.

When we are content, we can remain committed in difficult times regardless of how bad things may be or look. Not only should we learn the art of contentment, we should learn to stand. First Corinthians 15:58 (AMP) states, "Therefore, my beloved brothers and sisters, be steadfast, immovable, always excelling in the work of the Lord [always doing your best and doing more than is needed], being continually aware that your labor [even to the point of exhaustion] in the Lord is not futile nor wasted [it is never without purpose]." In other words, I want to go, but I have to stay. Or I want to stay, but I have to go. Being committed will be hard at times. But sometimes we are going to have to stand strong as we look over the faults and weaknesses of others as well as ourselves. We may have to reexamine or reevaluate how we feel about certain things. Buckle down and be committed in a hard and difficult place.

There are two old hymns, spiritual songs I fell in love with as young person, and I still love them. The first hymn is titled, "I Have Decided to Follow Jesus, no Turning Back." Enough said, no turning back no matter what. "Though none go with me, I still will follow, no turning back." The second hymn is titled, "On Christ the Sold Rock I Stand," by Edward Mote. I know everyone remembers singing that in Sunday school. I love the words of this hymn also because they speak about how we should put our trust ultimately and wholly in God, Jesus. Other things and people can fail you. I know in this life we have to trust others, but only to certain limits. When all else fails, or before it fails, ultimately you have to put your trust in God.

We all will be faced with difficult and trying times in this life, and during those times, the enemy of your soul wants you to think that you're alone and the only one going through various trials and the testing of your faith. But the Word of God reassures us that we are not the only ones going through these trials, and we are never alone, my friend. Christ told us, "Keep your lives free from the love of money and be content with what you have, because God has said, 'Never will I leave you; never will I forsake you'" (Hebrews 13:5). You can stand up, under, and in anything. You can overcome in victory and be committed in a difficult place by staying built up in the Lord and through his mighty Word.

Even John the Baptist, the forerunner of Christ Jesus, who came to bear witness to the coming of Christ, had a moment of remaining committed when things became difficult. A great man of God—John the Baptist—you might not think he would have a moment in life in which he was being committed in a hard and difficult place. But he did. John the Baptist, the cousin of Jesus, questioned his commitment to God the Father; Jesus; his faith; and the Christian movement, the Way. When John was faced with challenges during while he was in prison for evangelizing, preaching, and teaching about Jesus, he had to make a decision about remaining committed or bailing out and running for the hills. So don't shrink back. Hold true in your faith, and leap for it. "Beloved, do not be surprised at the fiery ordeal which is taking place to test you [that is, to test the quality of your faith], as though something strange or unusual were happening to you" (1 Peter 4:12 AMP).

The book of James says, "Consider it nothing but joy, my brothers and sisters, whenever you fall into various trials. Be assured that the testing of your faith [through experience] produces endurance [leading to spiritual maturity, and inner peace]. And let endurance have its perfect result and do a thorough work, so that you may be perfect and completely developed [in your faith], lacking in nothing" (James 1:2–4). Friend, you must not and should not forfeit the manifestation of blessings and promises of God by giving up and faint in difficult times. In Galatians 6:9, we are also reminded not to give up and become discouraged in doing well for at the proper time, we will reap if we do not faint and give in.

Chapter 1

HE CARES FOR ME

Casting all your cares [all your anxieties, all your worries, and all your concerns, once and for all] on Him, for He cares about you [with deepest affection, and watches over you very carefully].

—1 Peter 5:7 (AMP)

1 Peter 5:6–9
Psalm 27:10
Proverbs 3:5.
Romans 5:6–11
2 Corinthians 12:5–10

The love that our heavenly Father has for us is faithful. He promises to be there for us when no one else will be there. In Psalm 27:10–13 (AMP), King David stated,

Although my father and my mother have abandoned me, yet the Lord will take me up [adopt me as His child]. Teach me your way, O Lord, and lead me on a level path Because of my enemies [who lie in wait]. Do not give me up to the will of my adversaries, For false witnesses have come against me; They breathe out violence. I would have despaired had I not believed that I would see the goodness of the Lord In the land of the living. Wait for and confidently expect the Lord; be strong and let your heart take courage; yes, wait for and confidently expect the Lord.

Now that is an awesome love in King David's observation of how much God loved him. This key verse is very important in helping us also know the depth of God's love for us. I believe it is very important to know the value of God's love for us.

Be Grateful; God Cares

God cares for us so much that he will place people in our lives to help us through our difficult times. Reflect for a moment on someone who has stepped up to help you when it was needed. Someone who really had your back; Sometimes, without you even asking for help, God will send someone to step up and bless your life. Perhaps you may have been that person for someone in need, his or her ram in the bush. You may have been someone's backbone, stepping up and assisting when in need. Maybe you were someone's answer to the call for help during difficult times. When you think about it, you have to be grateful for the people God the Father placed in your life. The people who do not let you quit in the midst of trouble, who do not let you throw in the towel when things get tough, and when you do throw in the towel, they pick it up and throw it back at you. Through the care of God, I'm sure there have been people who did not allow you to give up or give in when things became difficult. We are to thank God for those who were faithful because of God's care. Maybe they were friends, family, associates, or neighbors. Hallelujah. Thank you, Father, for the people you have placed in our lives who do not let us quit and who help us bear our burdens.

I'm so grateful that we can take anything to God in prayer. There is nothing too big or too small to take to God the Father in prayer. We cast onto Jesus every burden, every care and uncertainty that we face in life because God cares for us. We should take our every need and concern to God in prayer. Not only does God the Father care for us, but if you look at this portion of scripture carefully, God wants us to humble ourselves and bring him every care and concern. God wants us to be self-disciplined, alert, cautious, and sober-minded at all times. He wants us to be firm in our faith, rooted and established, immovable, and know that we are not the only ones to resist the enemy.

But before we can resist the enemy, we have to humble ourselves unto God our Father and stop trying to do everything on our own. We have to trust and believe in him for everything. You will not be able to humble yourself under God until you realize what John 15 tells us, that apart from God we can do nothing. We need God the Father to live our best lives in this world. One of the first things we need to do is submit and surrender all to God. The main problem with most of us is not that God can't or won't help us. It's whether we allow him to help and bless us. Will we give God our issues? Will we give them up or over to him no matter what the issues are? The other problem is that we don't fully trust or believe God is willing and/or able to help, bless, save, deliver, and set us free. Unfortunately, we can be so self-reliant, so wrapped up in ourselves—our prideful selves—that we become foolish enough to think that we don't need God. And we neglect to call out to him. We are so blessed to have a God who cares for us even when we don't acknowledge him.

> While we were still helpless [powerless to provide for our salvation], at the right time Christ died [as a substitute] for the ungodly. Now it is an extraordinary thing for one to willingly give his life even for an upright man, though perhaps for a good man [one who is noble and selfless and worthy] someone might even dare to die. But God clearly shows and proves His own love for us, by the fact that while we were still sinners, Christ died for us. Therefore, since we have now been justified [declared free of the guilt of sin] by His blood, [how much more certain is it that] we will be saved from the wrath of God through Him. For if while we were enemies we were reconciled to God

through the death of His Son, it is much more certain, having been reconciled, that we will be saved [from the consequences of sin] by His life [that is, we will be saved because Christ lives today]. Not only that, but we also rejoice in God [rejoicing in His love and perfection] through our Lord Jesus Christ, through whom we have now received and enjoy our reconciliation [with God]. (Romans 5:6–11 AMP)

Trust, No Matter What

Mature people of God know how to remain standing in difficult times—regardless of what may be happening to or around them—because they trust or have learned to trust God the Father no matter what. Moses, Joseph, Ruth, King David, and even Job—just to name a few—were all people of great character who went through tremendous times of trouble and testing, but they remained faithful and committed. Perhaps you may know of someone who exercised great faith and remained committed in a hard place. Somehow God could trust them to do the right thing and come through hard and difficult times. Ask yourself as a Christian, "Can God trust me during difficulties? Can God trust me when he says no, not now, or wait? Do I trust God enough to help me in his perfect timing?" As a mature Christian, we must know how to be joyful in tribulation. Can God trust you with trouble, hurt, and pain, even though it may be your fault for the trouble? Will God be able to trust you to glorify him in the midst of your trouble until a breakthrough, deliverance, joy, or restoration comes? "Trust in the Lord with all your heart and lean not on your own understanding; in all your ways submit to him, and he will make your paths straight" (Proverbs 3:5).

Paul became a mighty man of God through trial and error. He came to understand God amid trouble. As Paul was faced with much tribulation, he learned to rely on and trust God. In his weakest moments, he discovered the strength of God. Paul realized that apart from God, he could truly do nothing. So he said he dare not boast. In his weakness he was made strong because he learned that God's grace was sufficient for him.

> I will boast about a man like that, but I will not boast about myself, except about my weaknesses. Even if I should choose to boast, I would not be a fool, because I would be speaking the truth. But I refrain, so no one will think more of me than is warranted by what I do or say, or because of these surpassingly great revelations. Therefore, in order to keep me from becoming conceited, I was given a thorn in my flesh, a messenger of Satan, to torment me. Three times I pleaded with the Lord to take it away from me. But he said to me, "My grace is sufficient for you, for my power is made perfect in weakness." Therefore I will boast all the more gladly about my weaknesses, so that Christ's power may rest on me. That's why,

for Christ's sake, I delight in weaknesses, in insults, in hardships, in persecutions, in difficulties. For when I am weak, then I am strong. (2 Corinthians 12:5–10)

Chapter 2

KNOW WHO YOU ARE; ACCEPT WHO YOU ARE

Daniel 10:19
1 Samuel 16:6–23; 17:17–26, 28–38
Jeremiah 29:11
James 4:7
Ephesians 4:23; 6:1–12
Psalm 139
2 Corinthians 10:4
Proverbs 3:16

One of the most amazing things Jesus demonstrated was that through all his suffering, he was able to stay focused. I believe Jesus was able to stay focused no matter what happened around him because he knew and accepted who he was, and he knew his purpose in life. Jesus accepted why he was here: to do his Father's will on earth. Because Jesus knew and accepted who he was and his purpose, he did not allow anything or anyone to distract him from his calling in life. He was committed to doing his Father's will first, even unto death. The Bible says Jesus stated that he and his Father were one: "I and the Father are one" (John 10:30). This one statement—"I and the Father are one"—is a powerful realization that Jesus made about himself, the acceptance of who he was. Jesus was reassured in this self-realization of who he was in the Father and his purpose in life. He had a powerful self-consciousness, no matter what. At that point, nothing and no one could have taken away his self-realization. I believe this is why some people were upset with Jesus, especially those who did not accept him and felt threaten by him.

The Pharisees and the Sadducees of Jesus's day were the high-society people, the upper crust, the movers and shakers of that day. Jesus did not go out of his way to impress or prove any point to the Pharisees and Sadducees. No one and nothing could make Jesus deny who he was and where he came from. The so-called high-society folk, the high priest, the politician, and powerful people must have wondered, *Well who does he think he is? Isn't that Mary and Joseph boy, the carpenter's son, Jesus of Nazareth? Yes, that's him. How dare he say he is the Son of the living God. He did not get our approval, and he did not come from our approved background, our class.* The Pharisees and Sadducees discussed among themselves, "We have to stop this Jesus of Nazareth with this nonsense before others begin to believe in what he is saying and follow him." Then they conspired against him to stop and ultimately kill him. They believed if they didn't stop him soon, they would have a problem on their hands.

These people felt so threatened by Jesus, his self-awareness, and his confidence of knowing and accepting who he was and his purpose that they even conspired about his death and burial. They even tried to deny and conceal his resurrection. Child of God, this is just how the enemy feels about you, especially when we are in difficult or challenging places in our lives. The enemy does not want you to know who you are, accept who you are and your purpose in this life, or accept God's plans for you. We must remember that the enemy comes to kill, steal, and destroy our lives and our purposes in life. The enemy knows this one truth about God's people: If they ever become aware and at peace with who they are, accept who they are, know and believe in their purposes in this life, they will be some powerful people. The enemy also knows that if God's people are committed in their purposes, even when it gets really hard, they will live victorious, powerful lives that bring God glory in the earthly realm.

Being Committed

First, in order to be committed in a hard, difficult place, I believe people need to know who they are, who they were created to be, their assignments, and their divine purposes in this life. Not only should one know who he or she is, one must accept it. To accept who one is means to know and accept he or she was created to be. It is my belief that too many people are unhappy and live unfulfilled lives because they cannot accept who God created them to be. They are locked in on believing the lies of the enemy, who whispers lies about them to defeat, destroy, and stop them from living out their divine purposes and best lives. If you don't know who you are, you will start believing the lies of the devil, your enemy. I believe it is a struggle many folk experience. When you know who you are, you will know what has the right to operate in your life and what does not. You will know the voice of God and what is from God and what's from the devil. The Word of God tells us that every good and perfect gift comes from God the Father. God said in Jeremiah 29:11 (AMP), "'For I know the plans and thoughts that I have for you,' says the Lord, 'plans for peace and well-being and not for disaster, to give you a future and a hope'."

Second, we need to be in agreement with what and who God the Father says we are. After we are in agreement with whom and what God says we are, we need to submit and surrender all to God. Not partial submission but all wholeheartedly given to God. James 4:7 tells us to "Submit yourselves, then, to God. Resist the devil, and he will flee from you." The key in this verse of scripture is to first summit and surrender to God the Father. Then you will be able to resist the devil. The Father said, "They will never follow a stranger, but will run away from him, because they do not know the voice of strangers" (John 10:5 AMP).

Third, one must know that "I will give thanks and praise to you, for I am fearfully and wonderfully made; Wonderful are your works, and my soul knows it very well" (Psalm 139:14 AMP). Accept that you were beautifully made of God the Father in his image and likeness. Even King David, with all of his mishaps, issues, and problems, loved God and accepted who he was and his purpose in life. Here we see a poor shepherd boy who would one day become king of a great nation. And although some did not see the greatness in King David, he saw the greatness in himself through the eyes of God. We have to see ourselves through God's eyes just as David did. In other words, *see yourself as God sees you, not as people see you.* People are fickle and change their minds as the weather changes. People will switch up on you quickly. As soon as their circumstances change, they will change. That is why we must put our ultimate trust in God. Why? Because one day people will go all out for you, and the very next day, they would say to crucify you. Isn't that what they did to Jesus? One day they were saying, "Hosanna, bless it be the name of the Lord." Then chapters later, when those same people encountered him the next time, they said, Crucify him." Yes, we have to put our trust in God.

David's father, Jesse, and his family did not recognize David as possibly becoming a king one day. Now that can be discouraging, but even that did not stop David. In Psalm 139:14, King David made a powerful statement about how he saw himself through the eyes of God. His self-consciousness and confidence came from God the Father. Again David said he would praise and thank his God because he knew he was fearfully and wonderfully made. That is an awesome statement of being in agreement with oneself through the eyes of God, a wonderful and loving God.

King David accepted himself because he knew God accepted and approved of him. He knew God loved him. David, a shepherd boy, was always overlooked, passed over, and ignored. But when the time came for God to promote and bring David to the forefront, nothing and no one could hold him back or stop him. Beloved, "what then shall we say to all these things? "If God is for us, who can be [successful] against us?" (Romans 8:31 AMP)

Loyalty and Commitment

Not only was David a person who learned the discipline of being committed in a hard place, Ruth was also such a person. Because Ruth knew and accepted who she was—unselfish, loyal, and committed—she was able to demonstrate her love toward someone else while living in a hard and difficult place. This beautiful story of loyalty and commitment takes place in the book of Ruth. While Ruth and her sister-in-law, Orpah, were dealing with being young widows, they took time to look after and care for Naomi, their mother-in-law, who was widowed also. These three women were committed to each other during a time when women were not considered to be of great importance or valued in mainstream society, especially without the presence of a male figure in the home.

Without a male in the household, Naomi decided to return to her hometown of Bethlehem. But before she set out, she tried to send her two daughters-in-law back to where they had come from, the land of Moab. (Ruth 1:8–9 tells us, AMP)Then Naomi said to her two daughters-in-law, 'Go back, each of you, to your mother's home. "May the Lord show you kindness, as you have shown kindness to your dead husbands and to me. May the Lord grant that each of you will find rest in the home of another husband." Then she kissed them goodbye and they wept aloud."

Vernadette R. Augustusel

Meaning in a Name

Ruth 1:11–18

"Ruth," a Moabite name, means "companion, friend, vision of beauty"; she was a symbol of loyalty and devotion. Ruth's name is also associated with special friendship. She was a special friend to her mother-in-law, Naomi, who became bitter due to the loss of not only her husband, Elimelech, but both of her sons, Chilion and Mahlon. Naomi's name meant "pleasing," but after the deaths of her sons, she asked to be called "Mara," which ironically means "bitter," which she became. Ruth was married to Mahlon, meaning "sickly"; Orpah was the wife of Chilion, meaning "wasting." Both sons' names were symbolic of their untimely deaths.

After Elimelech's death—whose name meant "My God is King"—his sons married Moabite women from Moab, a neighboring country. Neither of them had children by their wives. After the brothers' deaths, Orpah returned to her own people after escorting Naomi back to her hometown. Her name is supposed to be derived from the Hebrew word for "neck" (`oreph`) and so to mean "stiff-necked" because she turned away from following her mother-in-law. Others take it to mean "to turn back." Isn't that amazing? Orpah did just what her name meant; she turned back.

> But Naomi said, "Return home, my daughters. Why would you come with me? Am I going to have any more sons, who could become your husbands? Return home, my daughters; I am too old to have

another husband. Even if I thought there was still hope for me—even if I had a husband tonight and then gave birth to sons—would you wait until they grew up? Would you remain unmarried for them? No, my daughters, it is more bitter for me than for you, because the Lord's hand has turned against me!"

At this they wept aloud again. Then Orpah kissed her mother-in-law goodbye, but Ruth clung to her. "Look," said Naomi, "your sister-in-law is going back to her people and her gods. Go back with her." But Ruth replied, "Don't urge me to leave you or to turn back from you. Where you go I will go, and where you stay I will stay. Your people will be my people and your God my God. Where you die I will die, and there I will be buried. May the Lord deal with me, be it ever so severely, if even death separates you and me." When Naomi realized that Ruth was determined to go with her, she stopped urging her. (Ruth 1:11–18)

Ruth the Moabite

Ruth 3, 4

Since Naomi was of age and now a widow, she was not interested in ever being married again. But Ruth, another widow, was available for marriage. She was young, beautiful, and a loyal daughter-in-law of childbearing years. She had never had children to carry on the family's name and was available to remarry under the practice known as "Levirate marriage," which was the culture of Naomi's deceased husband practice. Under the Levirate marriage tradition, the brother of a deceased man was obligated to marry his brother's widow. "Levirate" is a derivative of the Latin word *Levir*, meaning "husband's brother."

Ruth did as her mother–in–law instructed her to do after gleaning and harvesting the fields of Boaz. Boaz was a wealthy landowner and one of Naomi's kinsman redeemers. A kinsman redeemer was one who kept the tradition of the Levirate marriage. In keeping with the Levirate marriage tradition during Naomi's day, the kinsman redeemer was required to avenge the death of a male relative, or in the case of one sold into slavery, he would pay the price for his release. However, if the man died before he had a child; the kinsman redeemer took the responsibility of marrying his relative's wife and father a child to bear his name.

As Naomi instructed Ruth, she placed herself one evening under Boaz's protection, submitting herself unto him, letting him know that she was willing for him to redeem her. It's is my belief that Ruth's loyalty and commitment caused her to be committed beyond her pain and difficulties. As Ruth's story goes on, she was blessed beyond measure due to her commitment and loyalty. God blessed Ruth so much because she showed kindness toward someone who had so little to offer in return and someone who had no way of paying her back.

With no hope and no restitution in sight, Naomi and

Ruth started their journey back to Naomi's homeland. They were destitute and in a hopeless situation, but Ruth was committed until the end. For the Word tells us in Proverbs 19:17, "whoever is kind to the poor, lends to the Lord, and he will reward them for what they have done." As noted previously, God blessed Ruth so much that she went on to marry one of Naomi's kinsman, Boaz. Afterward, Ruth became one of the wealthiest women of her time, and her offspring became an ancestor of Jesus Christ.

Staying Focused in a Faith Fight

First, you must know your enemy. And you must recognize your opponents, those who oppose you, and why they do so. Why are your enemies coming against you? What is the spirit behind them? We have to know how to battle in the spiritual realm: "blessed be the Lord, my Rock and my great strength, who trains my hands for war and my fingers for battle" (Psalm 144:1 AMP). We must also know our weapons and those of our enemy so we may know how to make war.

Second, one must be alert. First Peter 5:8 tells us, "Be alert and of sober mind. Your enemy the devil prowls around like a roaring lion looking for someone to devour." In other words, be aware, know and understand what kind of fight you are in, and know what resources are available for you to fight effectively. If you were in a physical fight in the natural realm, you would identify your opponent and recognize your best weapons of choice and available resources. The same awareness should occur in the spiritual realm; know who and how to fight the good fight of faith as things come up against you.

In order to be committed even in difficult times, we also must learn the art of staying focused. The enemy knows that if he can distract you, he can prevent you from going forth. The enemy fights dirty, and one of the main things he uses to prevent them going forth is distraction. Not only does he use distraction, he uses subtle distraction, so it is unnoticeable and undetected because one is unaware of its use. When dealing with distraction and the spirit of distraction, we must learn to be determined to stay focused if we are going to be committed. We don't have time to look all around in the wrong direction. Know the weapons God has given you so that you can stand up and fight against the spiritual attack of distractions. Distractions can cause one to look in the wrong direction or fight the wrong enemy. When striking the enemy, one must strike with precision and accuracy to cut the enemy down.

We must also remember that we are in spiritual warfare and must be dressed for battle. Ephesians 6:11 tells us, "Put on the full armor of God, so that you can take your stand against the devil's schemes." From time to time, we are going to engage in spiritual warfare. And when we do, it is our responsibility to know our enemies and the available weapons to fight the good fight of faith, all while staying focused and being committed. Second Corinthians 10:4 (AMP) says, "The weapons of our warfare are not physical [weapons of flesh and blood]. Our weapons are divinely powerful for the destruction of fortresses." Stay focused; don't be distracted by the negative and opposing forces around you. There are forces around you fighting for your attention to hinder you from your purpose and the will of God for your life.

My friend, keep pressing on. Don't be stagnant with distraction. Being distracted can mean a number of things. For example, one can be confused, frustrated, and/or worried. All these spirits will hook up and cause one to think irrationally. And that's just how the enemy wants you to be—confused. A confused state of mind that is full of worries is not a healthy mind. We must renew our minds and not spend our lives worrying. Remember, the enemy first comes up against the spiritual state of our minds. This is why God's Word tells us to be renewed in the spirit of our minds. Our minds have to be renewed with the Word daily to stay focused while committed in a hard place. And if your mind is not healthy, you are not healthy spiritually or physically. One should renew his or her mind because a healthy mind equals a healthy lifestyle. We read in Romans 12:2, "do not conform to the pattern of this world, but be transformed by the renewing of your mind. Then you will be able to test and approve what God's will is—his good, pleasing and perfect will," and where the mind goes, that is where our lives will go. We need to be aware and mindful of the state of our minds; be aware of where your mind is. Philippians 4:8 states, "finally, brothers and sisters, whatever is true, whatever is noble, whatever is right, whatever is pure, whatever is lovely, whatever is admirable—if anything is excellent or praiseworthy—think about such things."

Chapter 3

HOLD ON TO
YOUR FAITH

Galatians 6:9
Romans 5:3–4
James 1:2–6; 2:14–15
Psalm 100:4–5
John 16:32–33
1 Peter 4:12
2 Peter 1:5–8

"Let us not become weary in doing good, for at the proper time we will reap a harvest if we do not give up" (Galatians 6:9). How encouraging are those words in Galatians? In other words, hold on, stay the course. Don't quit because in due time, you will be blessed if you hang in there and hold on. Hold on to what you may be asking for. Hold on to what you believe and trust God the Father. Hold on to your faith, your faith in God, because you will face challenges from time to time in this life, especially during difficult or uncertain times. We find in John 16:32–33 (AMP),

> Jesus warred and reminded us of the fact that we will have trouble in this life, but he said to be encouraged because he was able to overcome the trouble he had faced in this world. So Jesus left us these words of encouragement. Take careful notice: an hour is coming, and has arrived, when you will all be scattered, each to his own home, leaving Me alone; and yet I am not alone, because the Father is with Me. I have told you these things, so that in Me you may have [perfect] peace. In the world you have tribulation and distress and suffering, but be courageous [be confident, be undaunted, be filled with joy]; I have overcome the world. [My conquest is accomplished, my victory abiding.]

Jesus, I believe, was able to be encouraged and to overcome for several reasons. First, Jesus knew God the Father and the Father's love for him. Second, Jesus also knew who he was and his purpose in life. Third, Jesus was not easily distracted; he was able to stay focused on his purpose in this life. And finally, Jesus accepted who he was created to be. No one else's opinion mattered about who God created him to be. When you know who you are, accept who you are, and know and accept the love of the Father for you, I believe you can overcome any and everything.

The closer Jesus got to the end of his journey in this life; he had to stay focused. And because he purposely remained focused, he was able to endure the cross and the crucifixion as things got really hard. During prayer and meditation time in the garden of Gethsemane, Jesus looked toward the heavens, prayed, cried out, "Father, if you are willing, take this cup from me; yet not my will, but yours be done" (Luke 22:42). At that point in his life, Jesus, in his humanity, had a moment of empowerment, where he had to be committed at a difficult time. He had to complete what he had come here for, even though it was at a most difficult time.

Yes, Jesus was facing a difficult time. But he trusted in the love he had for God the Father and the love he knew the Father had for him. Jesus knew his Father's love would strengthen and empower him to endure and bear up under his burden of being committed at a difficult time. In John 16:33, Jesus reminds us of the peace he has given us. And with the same peace, power, and strength that he had, we can endure anything and everything to complete any task we have in this life. "I have told you these things, so that in me you may have peace. In this world you will have trouble. But take heart! I have overcome the world" (John 16:33).

> Consider it nothing but joy, my brothers and sisters, whenever you fall into various trials. Be assured that the testing of your faith {through experience} produces endurance {leading to spiritual maturity, and inner peace. And let endurance have its perfect result and do a thorough work, so that you may be perfect and completely developed

{in your faith}, lacking in nothing}. (James
1:2–4 AMP)

From time to time, we all struggle in our faith as we
mature in our faith. Jesus was not the only one who had to
remain faithful at a difficult time. While in prison, John
the Baptist was also faced with being committed during
a difficult time. He struggled in his faith with little to no
hope. During his imprisonment, John the Baptist heard
about the things Jesus was doing and sent word to him
through his disciple. We read in Matthew 11:2 he asked,
"Jesus, are you the Messiah, or should we look for someone
else who will be the promised One?" Jesus responded by
giving John's disciple a list of the things he was doing and
had done, along with the instruction to "Go and report to
John what you have heard and seen: the blind receive their
sight and the lame walk; the lepers are cleansed by healing,
and the deaf hear; the dead are raised, and the poor have
the gospel preached to them. And blessed is he who does not
take offense at me, accepting me as the Messiah and trusting
confidently in my message of salvation."

So as James says, we all face issues and struggles in our
faith and in life. However, we should remain committed in
those difficult times.

Encouragement through the Word

Through reading and meditating on God's Word, our
Christian walk is strengthened. As we mature and grow as
Christians in our faith walk—spiritual journey—we will
learn how to endure and be committed even in difficult

23

times through learning and growing in the Word of God. I've found strength and empowerment by learning, studying, and applying God's Word in my daily life. The Word of God is alive and active, so let it be alive and active around and through you.

In 2 Peter 1:5–8 we are informed how to strengthen our faith and grow as mature Christians: "For this very reason, make every effort to add to your faith goodness; and to goodness, knowledge; and to knowledge, self-control; and to self-control, perseverance; and to perseverance, godliness; and to godliness, mutual affection; and to mutual affection, love; For if you possess these qualities in increasing measure, they will keep you from being ineffective and unproductive in your knowledge of our Lord Jesus Christ."

> Therefore, my beloved brothers and sisters, be steadfast, immovable, always excelling in the work of the Lord [always doing your best and doing more than is needed], being continually aware that your labor [even to the point of exhaustion] in the Lord is not futile nor wasted [it is never without purpose]. (1 Corinthians 15:58 AMP)

> Not that I speak from [any personal] need, for I have learned to be content [and self-sufficient through Christ, satisfied to the point where I am not disturbed or uneasy] regardless of my circumstances. I know how to get along and live humbly [in difficult times], and I also know how

to enjoy abundance and live in prosperity. In any and every circumstance I have learned the secret [of facing life], whether well-fed or going hungry, whether having an abundance or being in need. I can do all things [which He has called me to do] through Him who strengthens and empowers me [to fulfill His purpose—I am self-sufficient in Christ's sufficiency; I am ready for anything and equal to anything through Him who infuses me with inner strength and confident peace.] (Philippians 4:11–13 (AMP)

His anger is but for a moment,[a]His favor is for a lifetime. Weeping may endure for a night, But a shout of joy comes in the morning. (Psalm 30:5)

As the deer pants [longingly] for the water brooks, so my soul pants [longingly] for You, O God. My soul (my life, my inner self) thirsts for God, for the living God. When will I come and see the face of God? My tears have been my food day and night, While they say to me all day long, "Where is your God?" These things I [vividly] remember as I pour out my soul; How I used to go along before the great crowd of people and lead them in procession to the house of God [like a choirmaster before his singers, timing the steps to the music and the chant of the song], With the voice of joy and thanksgiving, a great crowd keeping a festival. Why are you in despair, O my soul? And why have you become restless and disturbed within me? Hope in God and wait expectantly for Him, for I shall again praise Him, for the help of His presence. O my God, my soul is in despair within me [the burden more than I can bear]; therefore I will [fervently] remember you from the land of the Jordan and the peaks of [Mount] Hermon, from Mount Mizar. Deep calls to deep at the [thundering] sound of your waterfalls; All Your breakers and Your waves have rolled over me. Yet the Lord will command His loving-kindness in the daytime, and in the night His song will be with me; a prayer to the God of my life. I will say to God my rock, "Why have you forgotten me? Why do I go mourning because of the oppression of the enemy?" As a crushing of my bones [with a sword], my adversaries taunt me, While they say continually to me, "Where is your God?" Why are you in despair, O my soul? Why have you become restless and disquieted within me? Hope in God and wait expectantly for Him, for I shall yet praise Him, The help of my countenance and my God. (Psalm 42:1–11 AMP)

Enter His gates with a song of thanksgiving And His courts with praise. Be thankful to Him, bless and praise His name. For the Lord is good; His mercy and loving-kindness are everlasting, His faithfulness [endures] to all generations. (Psalm 100:4–5 AMP)

Chapter 4

OPERATE IN PEACE: ALL IS WELL

2 Kings 4:8–36 (v. 26)
Mark 4:29
John 16:32–33
Colossians 3:15–16
Philippians 4:6–7
Isaiah 26:3
1 Peter 3:11
Thessalonians 3:16

> Let the peace of Christ rule in your
> hearts, since as members of one body you
> were called to peace. And be thankful.
> (Colossians 3:15)

I love this scripture because it tells me to let the peace of Christ have its power in my heart. This scripture also tells me that we have a choice in the matter of allowing and keeping the peace of God in our hearts and in our situation or to give up our peace to problems and trouble. In the midst of trouble, trying times, adversity, problems, and challenging times, one must learn the spiritual discipline— gift—of operating in peace. Operating in peace when chaos is all around you is possible, but for some, it can be very challenging. Keeping a clear head, calm emotions, and walking in peace during trying times are beneficial. It is vital to one's spiritual development simply because it demonstrates that you trust God, knowing that he is with you and all will be well. Isaiah 26:3 reminds us that God will keep you in perfect peace if your mind is set. So stay focused on him and steadfast in your thinking of him and his goodness.

Operating in peace is a form of worship as you experiences his very presence within, around, and among you. I believe God's peace ushers in his presence among us. Our hearts and minds are also guarded when we trust God and operate in peace, his peace. We must guard our hearts and minds because out of them, the Bible says, flows the issues of life. In life, we sometimes experience adversity, problems, and trouble sent from the enemy that is designed to distract and/or destroy us. We must guard our hearts and emotions so that the issues of life don't have power over us. Purposely walking in peace during adverse times guards you from operating in anger, hopelessness, bitterness, and retaliation. Believe it or not, when the presence of God is invited into a situation through practicing the spiritual discipline of operating peace, a sense of his presences will reassure and enforce you with strength and power to move on, even stand during adversity.

It is believed that one of the ways we worship God is through the practice of peace. Peace has the power and evidence of God's love and presence. Just like Jesus told the storm in Mark 4:39, "He got up, rebuked the wind and said to the waves, 'Quiet! Be still!' Then the wind died down and it was completely calm." We must remember to speak peace and operate in it whenever the storms of life start blowing into our lives. We know storms can disrupt things, so learn to handle the storms of life like Jesus did by speaking and operating in peace. And wherever God's love and presence are, there will always be victory. This is why Jesus said, "Peace I leave with you; My [perfect] peace I give to you; not as the world gives do I give to you. Do not let your heart be troubled, nor let it afraid," (John 14:27 AMP).

No one can take God's peace from you, but you can give it up or give it away. The choice is yours to keep God's peace and hold on to it—or not. Hold on to the peace that God gave you, and don't allow anything or anyone to steal it from you. As a matter of fact, go after your peace. First Peter 3:11 tells us to seek peace and pursue it: "They must turn from evil and do good; they must seek peace and pursue it." In other words, seek God and pursue him. Worship him within the state of being peaceful and operating in peace. When going after your peace, be determined to have it and keep it. The peace of God is yours to keep.

While Jesus was talking to his disciples he told them of troubling times that were coming and that they would feel as if they were alone in the world. However, he reassured them that they would never be alone. In the midst of trouble you may feel alone at times, but God the Father promises to be with you. Have you ever felt alone in the world when facing problems and troubles? In this world, Jesus told the disciples that they would have troubles and problems, but not to worry and to take courage and be confident for he overcame the world and its troubles due to the perfect peace of God. The term "perfect" here means mature. Jesus had mature peace. Notice how he remained calm in horrible times; we can operate in that type of mature peace too. This type of peace is anointed to withstand anything that comes. The mature peace Jesus possessed does not mean his state of being peaceful was not without its challenges, but the peace Jesus had was anointed, supernatural, and powerful. Jesus, operating in peace, was the very embodiment of God's presence, God in the flesh. Jesus had mature peace for two reasons: (1) because he recognized and understood that the peace he possessed came from God the Father, and he had a choice to keep it. And (2) Jesus also trusted and had confidence in the peace of God. He knew that the peace he possessed had been tested, tried, and proven to bring him through any trial or trouble he faced: "A time is coming and in fact has come when you will be scattered, each to your own home. You will leave me all alone. Yet I am not alone, for my Father is with me. I have told you these things, so that in me you may have peace. In this world you will have trouble. But take heart! I have overcome the world" (John 16:32–33).

Vernadette R. Augustusel

It Is Well with My Soul

2 Kings 4:26–36

As one who has experienced great trials in life, I believe knowledge of God's supernatural peace is essential. With God's supernatural peace, there is a reassurance of God's presence in our midst, letting us know all will be well, no matter what you may have encountered or the outcome you may have had to face. Even in troubling and testing times of one's faith, God's peace is available to anyone who looks for it, calls on it, and believes in it.

There's an old hymn that I love titled "When Peace like a River," by Horatio Gates Spafford. In 1873, Spafford was a prominent American lawyer, a church leader, and an elder in the Presbyterian Church. In Spafford's life, he was faced with one tragedy after another, yet became aware and took hold of the supernatural peace of God amid those challenges and trying times. It is the God kind of peace that Philippians 4:7 speaks of: "And the peace of God [that peace which reassures the heart, that peace] which transcends all understanding, [that peace which] stands guard over your hearts and your minds in Christ Jesus [is yours]."

I first loved this hymn because of its lyrics, which really spoke to me. After researching the reasons for this hymn and the life behind it, I appreciated and loved it even more. Two years after the death of his four-year-old son from scarlet fever, Spafford lost four more children in a shipwreck when his family was on its way to a Europe vacation. Spafford's wife and their four daughters were going on a holiday ahead of him. Only Spafford's wife survived the shipwreck. Despite the tragedies, this giant of a man in the Christian faith he chose to write a hymn that spoke of the supernatural peace he possessed. The hymn goes as follows.

When peace like a river attendeth my way,
when sorrows like sea billows roll;
whatever my lot, thou hast taught me to say,
"It is well, it is well with my soul."

Refrain (may be sung after final stanza only):
It is well with my soul;
it is well, it is well with my soul.

Though Satan should buffet, though trials should come,
let this blest assurance control:
that Christ has regarded my helpless estate,
and has shed his own blood for my soul.

Refrain

My sin oh, the bliss of this glorious thought!
my sin, not in part, but the whole,
is nailed to the cross, and I bear it no more;
praise the Lord, praise the Lord, O my soul!

Refrain

O Lord, haste the day when my faith shall be sight,
the clouds be rolled back as a scroll;

the trump shall resound and the Lord shall
descend;
even so, it is well with my soul." It is well
with my soul;
it is well, it is well with my soul.

In the middle of all that Spafford went through, he was
able to sing. And because of Spafford's faith in God and the
supernatural peace he possessed, as he passed over the spot
where he lost his four daughters when the ship went down,
he began to write, "When peace like a river attendeth my
way, when sorrows like sea billows roll," and continued until
he had written those great words, "It is well with my soul."
Phil Bliss, a composer friend of Spafford's, put a tune to his
words, naming it after the ship, *Ville DU Havre.* This hymn
tells us of a peace that is comforting and reassuring during
times of trouble, spiritual crisis, and uncertain times in our
lives. Peace can give us hope amid struggles and chaos, and
in trying times.

Let the [spoken] word of Christ have its
home within you [dwelling in your heart
and mind—permeating every aspect of
your being] as you teach [spiritual things]
and admonish and train one another with
all wisdom, singing psalms and hymns and
spiritual songs with thankfulness in your
hearts to God. (Colossians 3:16 AMP)

The Lord is my strength and my defense;
he has become my salvation. Shouts of joy
and victory resound in the tents of the

righteous: "The Lord's right hand has done mighty things!" (Psalm 118:14–15)

As I think back to a time when I was going through a family crisis, dealing with children becoming teenagers, medical issues, and financial issues all at once, I remember leaving church one day, and a sister came over to me. She said, "Just get a song, begin to sing your way through everything you are going through, and things will get better, my sister." Then she just walked away. Well this old hymn "It Is Well" is one of those hymns that reminds me of how good and great God is. Worship through a song in your heart to God will always ease the pains of life. Worship will always bring calm to the sea of life, especially when one is facing frustration, worry, and troubles from all over the place.

A few years ago, I wrote a book titled *Don't Worry, Worship, Worship Don't Worry*. In this book I explained and reminded folks of times when and how one should worship their ways through any and every challenge in life, especially during difficult times. Even King Saul would call on David to play for him when he was going through something trying. As a matter of fact, it has been said that problems and troubles during difficult times can actually promote spiritual maturity and usher you into the presence of God. Sometime crises, problems, and issues bring us to where God would have us to be and help us to carry out his plans and purposes for our lives. Sometimes we won't find peace in the midst of silence and calmness, but the peace that God gives is so powerful it can even be present among uncertainty, chaos, and trouble, causing one to be still, at peace, with inner peace, and knowing it is well or will be well.

Chapter 5

LOVE WALK, POWER WALK

1 Corinthians 13:4–8
1 John 4:4, 8, 18
Mark 12:28–34
Matthew 22:37
Romans 5:2–5; 13:8–10
Galatians 5:6, 13–23
Leviticus 19:18
Ephesians 3:16–19
Psalms 51:10; 107:20
Proverbs 4:23

The Power of Love

> You shall not take revenge nor bear any
> grudge against the sons of your people, but
> you shall love your neighbor (acquaintance,

associate, and companion) as yourself; I am the Lord. (Leviticus 19:18)

True Love, the God Kind of Love

1 Corinthians 13:4–8 (AMP)

What is love? Well according to the Word of God, love is several things, but it is constant and steadfast during difficult times. I believe we have a good picture of what true love is in 1 Corinthians 13:4–8 (AMP):

> If I speak with the tongues of men and of angels, but have not love [for others growing out of God's love for me], then I have become only a noisy gong or a clanging cymbal [just an annoying distraction]. And if I have the gift of prophecy [and speak a new message from God to the people], and understand all mysteries, and [possess] all knowledge; and if I have all [sufficient] faith so that I can remove mountains, but do not have love [reaching out to others], I am nothing. If I give all my possessions to feed the poor, and if I surrender my body to be burned, but do not have love, it does me no good at all. Love endures with patience and serenity, love is kind and thoughtful, and is not jealous or envious; love does not brag and is not proud or arrogant. It is not rude;

it is not self-seeking, it is not provoked [nor overly sensitive and easily angered]; it does not take into account a wrong endured. It does not rejoice at injustice, but rejoices with the truth [when right and truth prevail]. Love bears all things [regardless of what comes], believes all things [looking for the best in each one], hopes all things [remaining and endures all things [without weakening]. Love never fails [it never fades nor ends]." But as for prophecies, they will pass away; as for tongues, they will cease; as for the gift of special knowledge, it will pass away.

I believe God is calling us to a radical love walk regardless of where we are and what we have to face in this life. The Word of God tells us that God poured his abundant love into our hearts through the Holy Spirit. We become helpless and in a difficult state; because we do not taped into the love of God available to us in our hearts. That love we have access to is the ultimate power and authority of God in our lives. The love that God has for us is so awesome nothing can stop it from reaching us, no pain or suffering. Hallelujah! I can't stop praising God the Father for his unfailing love; it's so encouraging. We read in Romans 5:2–5 (AMP),

Through Him we also have access by faith into this [remarkable state of] grace in which we [firmly and safely and securely] stand. Let us rejoice in our hope and the confident assurance of [experiencing and enjoying] the glory of [our great] God [the manifestation of His excellence and power]. And not only this, but [with joy] let us exult in our sufferings and rejoice in our hardships, knowing that hardship (distress, pressure, trouble) produces patient endurance; and endurance, proven character (spiritual maturity); and proven character, hope and confident assurance [of eternal salvation]. Such hope [in God's promises] never disappoints us, because God's love has been abundantly poured out within our hearts through the Holy Spirit who was given to us.

Now that we have an idea of what love is, look at what love is not. It is not manipulation, deceitful, hateful, jealous, or envious. Love has no strife, rebellion, discord, control, greed, betrayal, or selfishness. Love is a spirit, and the Bible says that God is love: "Whoever does not love does not know God, because God is love" (1 John 4:8). So the presence of almighty God, the spirit of love, has power and authority. As we allow the power of God's love to flow through our lives, we can experience joy and excitement for living. Like the old song says, "This joy that I have, the world did not give it to me and the world cannot take it away." Well, this love that I have the world did not give to me, and it sure can't take it away.

The love of God will always bring victorious living. When people become aware of God's love, they experience a sense of peace, an unexplainable sense of peace. So many people don't have a zeal for living. They just go through life, existing from one day to the next, simply because they do not realize how much God loves them and how much he wants his love to flow in and through them.

God's love is one of the first spiritual gifts to humanity. But most of us do not acknowledge the depth of God's love simply because we don't realize that it is a spiritual force with power, anointing, and abilities. And because we have not acknowledged God's love, we cannot operate in God's power and the authority he has given us on the earth. What we need to do is give up our hang-ups, get together, and serve God and each other through the spiritual force of love. If we just understood that when we are not loving but scheming, plotting, backbiting, and harboring jealousy and hatred toward each other, for example, the kingdom of darkness advances in our lives and in the earthly realm. But if we learn to walk in God's love, the kingdom of heaven advances. One quick question. Whose side are you on? Let's get together on kingdom business and work on bringing the kingdom of God here on earth. When we are not walking in God's love, his Spiritual force, we are actually working against him and his kingdom. Either we are for God by walking in his love, his Spirit, his force, or we are working for Satan, harboring ill feelings and operating in evilness. Again, whose side are you on?

The fruit of the Spirit is love. A good example of walking in God's love is in Galatians 5:22–23: "but the fruit of the Spirit is love, joy, peace forbearance, kindness, goodness, faithfulness, gentleness and self-control. Against such things there is no law." We are reminded of what the fruit of the

Spirit is and what it will produce if we walk in it. In other words, if we cultivate the love of God in our lives. We have to cultivate our love walk daily. We cultivate our love through prayer, learning, and knowing the Word of God. Prayer helps us to cultivate the fruit of the Spirit so that we may grow spiritually. Operating in God's love and practicing it also helps us to grow spiritually. There are many forces— spirits—that try to destroy us spiritually. John 10:10 says, "the thief comes only to steal and kill and destroy; I have come that they may have life and have it to the full." So since the enemy, Satan, comes into our lives to kill, steal, and destroy our lives. We must remember that Jesus said that he comes into our lives so we may enjoy life and have it more abundantly. God gives us the ability to love unlovable people during difficult times. Dealing with difficult people can be challenging, but we can still operate in God's love and not give in to the evilness of others while in a difficult place. No matter what.

Sometimes in this life we face difficulties, difficult people, hard places, situations, and circumstances. But we must remember the words of Jesus and the love of God because God wants us to win and be victorious in life. However, while we agree with God that he loves us and want us to win regardless, we are dealing with spirits of depression, heaviness, bitterness, illness, unforgiveness, sickness, infirmity, hated, anger, hopelessness, and fear at the same time. All these spirits try to steal our joy, peace, and love. But even amid difficulties and uncertainties, we can still have the presence of God and his peace, his joy, and his love with us because we have his spirit, the Holy Spirit, living inside us. The evidence of his presence is with us through the Holy Spirit versus the sinful nature. If we say that we belong to Christ, then we have crucified the lust of the flesh, our sinful nature.

We must find our way back to love. However, our old nature, our flesh, does not want to operate in God's love. But we have the power to bring ourselves into submission, in line with God's Spirit, evidence of his love in us by the fruit of the Spirit, love. The fruit of the spirit, love, will produce joy, peace, patience, kindness, goodness, faithfulness, gentleness, and self-control. Everything God the Father wants to teach us is based wholly on love—God's love for us, our love for him, our love for each other, and our love for self. But remember, self-love is not selfishness. This is also why the Word of God reminds us that the greatest commandment to keep is to walk in love, to love thy neighbor as you love yourself. Without love we have nothing because anything absent from love is without God. God is love. The very existence of God is exemplified in love. Everything in the kingdom is based on love. We have nothing without love, not even access to kingdom benefits and blessings. In Matthew 22:34–40, when Jesus was being questioned about which of the commandments was the greatest, he told the religious teachers that the greatest of all commandments is to walk in love. And believe it or not, your love walk is just where your healing is, your blessings, your peace, and your prosperity, even as your soul prospers. It's all connected to our love walk.

> But if you are guided *and* led by the Spirit, you are not subject to the Law. Now the practices of the-sinful nature are clearly

evident: they are sexual immorality, impurity, sensuality (total irresponsibility, lack of self-control), idolatry, sorcery, hostility, strife, jealousy, fits of anger, disputes, dissensions, factions [that promote heresies], envy, drunkenness, riotous behavior, and other things like these. I warn you beforehand, just as I did previously, that those who practice such things will not inherit the kingdom of God. But the fruit of the Spirit [the result of His presence within us] is love [unselfish concern for others], joy, [inner] peace, patience [not the ability to wait, but how we act while waiting], kindness, goodness, faithfulness, gentleness, self-control. Against such things there is no law. And those who belong to Christ Jesus have crucified the sinful nature together with its passions and appetites. If we [claim to] live by the [Holy] Spirit, we must also walk by the Spirit [with personal integrity, godly character, and moral courage—our conduct empowered by the Holy Spirit]. We must not become conceited, challenging *or* provoking one another, envying one another. (Galatians 5:18–26 AMP)

Now I ask you, how we can say that we are for God and not be walking in the fruit of the Spirit, which is the power of God's love? How can we say we know him and not practice his presences by walking in his love? When we practice love, we are practicing his presence. As we practice the fruit of the Spirit, love, and being in God's presence, we will experience other spirits such as joy, peace, kindness, and everything that is good. The entire Word of God is summed up in a single command, love: "for the entire law is fulfilled in keeping this one command: 'Love your neighbor as yourself" (Galatians 5:14). Friend, examine your love walk. If someone is walking in hatred, envy, deceit, and greed, among others, that person's love walk is out of order. Where is the love? Get back in line with God, and start practicing his presence by walking in love. So many of us miss out on the greatest love affair of a lifetime because; we don't acknowledge God's love and don't operate in his love. We must examine ourselves and allow the love of God to flow in and through our lives.

Oh, by the way, God play for keeps. He is not looking for any part-time loves. So if you're thinking of skipping out on God and two-timing him, it's best that you don't mess over him in any way because you cannot mock God. We need to be consumed by the love of God or leave it alone. Just as Jesus was a living example of God's love, we are to be examples of his love as well.

Our love walk is very important to our Christian walk and spiritual growth. The more of God's love we walk in, the more we grow spiritually. As we walk in God's love, the evidence of his presence and power are made manifest in and through our lives. If we allow God into our lives, love can and will transform us. As more of the transformation takes place, we become more like him. God intends us to be transformed into his image more and more. It is my belief that the more we yield to the spirit of love, the more we walk in the power of God. And the power of God's love will turn our lives completely around. The Word says it is the goodness of the Lord that causes us to repent. God's goodness demonstrates his love toward us. This love, once experienced, will cause one to become a new person, a better person in Christ Jesus. As we allow God's love to transform us, his power will flow in and through our lives to change things for the better, which will eventually help us to be committed in a hard and difficult place.

Our love walk will always affect our quality of life and how well and how long we live. Some people have literally died from a broken heart; they felt as though no one truly loved them. Perhaps they never experienced how to love God or themselves. Sadly, they did not come to know and understand that God's love was available to them. Love is a very important part of life. As we develop spiritually and physically, it is very important that we experience love. But most important, we need to experience God's love. It is my belief that if someone were raised in an atmosphere of love, or maybe experienced love later in life, he or she would have a healthy lifestyle. Healthy emotions and a sense of well-being, I believe, are signs of someone who has experienced love and care. People who have been abused emotionally, mentally, and/or physically are often afraid to love because they don't know if they can ever trust themselves to love again. They are afraid of being hurt all over again. Trust is a major part of love, and folks who have been hurt don't want to hurt anymore. To keep from being hurt again from the lack of love, they put up defense mechanisms to guard their hearts and feelings from being hurt. So many people today are afraid to and fearful of love. But fear is our enemy for God said that he did not give us a spirit of fear: "For God did not give us a spirit of timidity or cowardice or fear, but [He has given us a spirit] of power and of love and of sound judgment and personal discipline [abilities that result in a calm, well-balanced mind and self-control]" (2 Timothy 1:7). The Word of God also tells us to remember that "There is no fear in love. But perfect love drives out fear, because fear has to do with punishment. The one who fears is not made perfect in love" (1 John 4:18). Some people who are afraid to love desire and want to love more than anything, but they are in a prison from past hurt and refuse to walk in love or allow themselves to be loved. They see no way of ever getting out of the prison of no love.

Dear friend, there is a way out, and it is through the precious blood of Jesus Christ. Jesus is the way, the truth and the light. The light of God's love shines through the darkness in your soul and guides you towards true love, God's love. God's love came to set the captives free. As the Word says, whomever Jesus sets free is free indeed. You may ask yourself how I can get out of this prison of no love. Just call on the name of the Lord Jesus right where you are. Ask him for help. Be truthful with him, and be truthful with yourself. Tell him that you want out, and you want to love again or experience true love for the very first time. Tell him that you need to experience love and give love but that you don't know how or where to begin. As you open yourself to love, you must understand that pain and hurt may come again. But allow yourself to be loved and give love as if no one has or will ever hurt you again. Allow God's love to flow in and through your life. Be a vessel of his love. We must learn to overlook people's offenses because if we don't, we will walk around in the bondage and pain of others' hurting us. And most of us have heard the saying that, "Hurting people hurts people." So some people have the mentality, "I'm going to hurt them before they hurt me." Every day practice overlooking the pain someone is or may be trying to cause you. Don't allow the spirits of frustration and aggravation interfere with your love walk. There are spirits that will try to stop you from operating in the love of God. Walk in love regardless, and learn to forgive. This will keep you free from the spirit of offense. In other words, learn to forgive as much as possible. Remember, the Word of God tells us, "Above all else, guard your heart, for everything you do flows from it" (Proverbs 4:23). We should not harbor ill feelings in our hearts and minds. Remember that in the spiritual realm, our minds and hearts are one in the same. As a man or woman thinks in the heart, so does he or she: "For as he thinks in his heart, so is he [in behavior—one who manipulates]. He says to you, 'Eat and drink,' Yet his heart is not with you [but it is begrudging the cost]" (Proverbs 23:7 AMP).

Here is a famous quote from Marcus Aurelius, an emperor of ancient Rome: "a man's life is what his thoughts make of it." Therefore, we should keep our hearts clear and pure because this is what God loves and looks for. Ask God the Father to "create in you a clean heart and renew a right spirit within you," just like King David did in Psalm 51:10. God honored and blessed King David because he was honest and truthful with where his heart was.

Once you are out of the prison of no love, you must make sound decisions and be determined to never going back behind those bars of imprisonment. Fight for your freedom to love and be loved because it is a daily battle. Every day of your life you will be faced with the choice of holding on to pain and hurt from your past and present or to walk in love. Sometimes others will bring you their pains and hurts just to cause you pain and hurt. But reject it, and show the depth of God's love, even to those who mean you no good. The power of God's love can conquer all things, but we must have faith in it. The Bible tells us that it is impossible to please God without faith. Well, faith in what? We must have faith in the power of God's love, which is real. If we do not exercise faith in the power of God's love, it cannot and will not work for us. We need love for our faith to work, and we need faith for our love to work. Without love and faith together, neither will work. Love and faith, both are needed in order to work.

For us to be committed to anything, we need faith and love, especially when we are faced with daily life issues. Each day we must make a choice to do something with our pains and hurts. What are you going to do with yours? Are you going to exercise your faith and release pain and hurt to God, or are you going to hold on to it? Will you begin each day with a commitment to walk in God's love or go back to the prison of no love? Friend, you must fight the good fight of faith, and stay free to walk in God's love. We walk in God's love by daily communicating with him through prayer and reading and meditating on God's Word. Spend some time with him so that you can be empowered to walk in God's love. This is the only way to stay free to love God's way. To walk in God's love is to walk in the supernatural. And we walk in the supernatural again through prayer and reading and meditating on his Word. If you try to love in your ability, you will fail to love. But remember, God's love is a powerful force that will never fail. His love is his spirit and his presence that is alive and active and helps and empowers us to love when love seems impossible, especially when being committed in a hard, difficult place.

We can walk in God's love and move by his power in several ways:

1. Be aware of your inner person/your spiritual person. We need to be aware of where we are spiritually. Make a daily assessment of where you are spiritually and be truthful with yourself. If something is not right in your spirit, go to God in prayer. Repent and he will help you to get yourself together.

2. Be committed to daily devotions through prayer and reading and studying the Word of God. Commune with him on a daily basis. Meditate on his love for you and his promises. Listen to the Word. Speak and confess the Word over yourself.

3. Submit and surrender to God the Father all ill feelings you may be harboring. Cleanse your heart daily. Psalm 51:10 reminds us to ask God to create in us a clean heart and renew a right spirit within. This was King David's prayer to God. In order for God to pour his love into our hearts, they must be cleansed and surrendered to him. Keep dumping your heart out to God daily. God's love cannot come into a heart wanting to hold on to or is filled with ill feelings and evilness. Make sure you desire or have a heart that is pleasing to God. And if it's not pleasing

to God, ask him to come into your heart and clean it out because you want a pure heart. That pleases God for God the Father is looking for those who want a pure heart that is pleasing to him. Believe it or not, apart from God, we can do nothing, even having a pure heart for him. In (John 15:5 AMP) Jesus said, "I am the Vine; you are the branches. The one who remains in Me and I in him bears much fruit, for [otherwise] apart from Me [that is, cut off from vital union with me] you can do nothing."

4. Walk in forgiveness. Practice being kind to others. Learn to smile and to laugh again. "Lift up your heads, you gates; be lifted up, you ancient doors that the King of glory may come in. who is this King of glory? The Lord strong and mighty, the Lord mighty in battle. Lift up your heads, you gates; lift them up, you ancient doors, that the King of glory may come in (Psalm 24:7–9). So lift up your head and live again; there is always something to live for. The Word of God also says in Ecclesiastes 9:4, "anyone who is among the living has hope –even a live dog is better off than a dead lion."

5. Cast your cares and anxieties on God the Father daily. "Cast all your cares on him because he cares for you" (1 Peter 5:7). "Rejoice always, pray continually, give thanks in all circumstances; for this is God's will for you in Christ Jesus" (1 Thessalonians 5:16–18).

6. Learn to trust God to help you to love the unlovable. Remember to ask him to help you, and walk in his love. Practice, practice, practice walking in love

because practice makes perfect. In other words, practice brings about maturity in a thing. So the more you practice your love walk, the more mature you become in love. Never give up. Always keep trying to walk in love.

7. Remember love never fails, and understand that if we give love and sow love, love will find its way back to us. We always reap what we have sown.

Lord, Teach Us How to Love

> I pray that out of his glorious riches he may strengthen you with power through his Spirit in your inner being, so that Christ may dwell in your hearts through faith. And I pray that you, being rooted and established in love, may have power, together with all the Lord's holy people, to grasp how wide and long and high and deep is the love of Christ, and to know this love that surpasses knowledge—that you may be filled to the measure of all the fullness of God.
>
> —Ephesians 3:16–19

At one time in my life, when I believed that I was walking in the God kind of love, the Word of God opened up to me and revealed that I really was not as loving and lovable as I thought I was. Scriptures, the Word of God, help us to understand that God's ways are truly not our ways. I realized that in order for us to walk and operate in

God's love, we must first know and understand what the God kind of love is and what we have come to understand and know love to be. If we were to size ourselves according to the definition of love in and throughout God's Word, we would live in victory more often than in defeat because God's, "love never fails" (1 Corinthians 13:8).

Too often we come to believe that love is for weak people and wimps, but that is not so. A fearless person is one who walks in love. Fearless people are not afraid to love. Remember, "there is no fear in love, but perfect love drives out fear, because fear has to do with punishment. The one who fears is not made perfect in love" (1 John 4:18". Fear, the Bible says, has torment, and we know we don't have to be fearful in being committed in a hard and difficult place with the power of God's perfect love. With God's powerful, perfect love, we can face anything, person, or situation.

There are misconceptions about a person walking in love. People walking in love are not weak, fearful, timid, or pushovers. I say this again. One of the greatest and most powerful people to have ever lived was Jesus Christ, and he continuously walked in the God kind of love. Walking in love is not always easy, but it is rewarding and worthwhile. It takes strength to walk in love. A person operating in God's love is someone who is courageous and has self-control. Being able to walk in love takes someone who's secure in who he or she is and can hold one's peace amid confusion, trouble, and difficult times. A person demonstrating love is someone who can walk in forgiveness toward folks who are deliberately trying to hurt the individual, causing pain.

Actually, Christian love is one of the highest forms of spiritual warfare. This is why God commands and reminds us to walk in it. People operating in God's love will not wimp out under pressure. When someone mistreats a person operating in God's love, that individual won't retaliate because he or she knows and understands that one's inner person will be strengthened to operate in God's love and his power of forgiveness. A person who walks in God's love will stand up for the truth and tell the truth in love while knowing and believing God's love will protect him or her. Wimps would not and could not allow folks to strip them naked in front of their communities, hang them on a cross or tree, and kill them for something they did not do. That type of situation would take supernatural strength to handle. It would take the God kind of love to stand in all that. If Jesus wanted to, he could have come down off that cross and whipped—even killed—a lot of his accusers and abusers. Most of us don't realize that God's love has supernatural strength that empowers you with supernatural abilities. This kind of love can forgive those who oppose you every chance they get just because they can or want to. This kind of love can give until it hurts to those who despitefully use them because they trust in, rely on, and look to God's love to reward them down the road for what they have done.

Love is the foundation of all things that are godly. Without love you have nothing. And because God is love, without God you have nothing. Not only is love a spiritual force and God's presence, love is also a choice and an action. If we choose to walk in love, we will open up to God's spirit. When we walk in love, we walk in God, his power, his characteristics, and his anointing. God showed his love to us by dying on the cross for sins he did not commit. God came down from heaven in bodily form as Jesus Christ and bore our sins, curses, sicknesses, and filthy conditions so that we may have abundant lives and eventually, eternal life. Now that's love! God did not have to do that, but he chooses to because of his love for humanity, his creation.

Love Language

In the Hebrew language there are three languages for love. These love languages are different in meaning for the term love. Raya—which basically means friend is the first word used to describe love in the Hebrew language, (Song of Songs 4:7) In Song of Songs Raya is also known as companion, best friend, companion and/or soul mate. Ahav—the root word of Ahava—is the second term in Hebrew for love, which means deep affection, committed/ devoted love. With Ahav type of love it is more about giving love, then receiving devoted love, (Song of Songs 8:7). Finally, the third Hebrew term for love is Dod—means to show passion, romantic feelings, physical, sexual in nature. Dod also means to fondle or carouse (Song of Songs 1:2).

The Three Dimensions of Love

The first dimension of love is agape. It is a Greek term that best describes the God kind of love. It is the purest form of love, which is a divine love. Agape is the gift of love God has for humanity. It is not characterized by desires, attractions, or needs.

Philia, the second dimension of love, is characterized as a friendship or brotherly love that humans desire and give to each other. Love of desire or of a sexual nature is known as eros. Eros is the third dimension of love and is mainly physical (Bowden, Richardson 341–342).

Not only are there three dimensions of love, there are also several types of love. When we say we "love," we can mean any number of things. John Lee, in 1973/1974, developed a widely cited approach to love. Lee suggested that there are six styles of love.

1. Eros—Love of beauty, powerful physical attraction, and sexual desire
2. Mania—Obsessive love, jealousy, possessiveness, and intense love, dependency
3. Ludus—Playful love, carefree, casual, fun-and-games approach
4. Storge—Companionate love, peaceful, affectionate, love based on mutual trust and respect
5. Agape—Altruistic love, self-sacrificing, kind, and patient love; God's kind of love, divine love
6. Pragma—Practical love, sensible, realistic (Benokraitis 119)

After viewing the different dimensions and types or forms of love, now let us look again at what God's Word says about love. In 1 Corinthians 13:4–8, the Word says, "That love is patient, love is kind. It does not envy, it does not boast, it is not proud. It is not rude, it is not self-seeking, it is not easily angered and it keeps no record of wrongs. Love does not delight in evil but rejoice with the truth. It always protects, always trusts, always hopes and always perseveres. Love never fails." Wow! The love of God is really something.

Now if we were to carefully read God's definition of love and be very truthful with ourselves, we would have to admit that we all have issues to work on concerning our love walks.

One day as my husband and I were really going through a difficult time, we had this big argument about something stupid in which I learned a lesson about love. The Holy Spirit can really teach you about the things of God and about where you are—if you allow him to, the third person of the trinity. The Trinity: the Godhead, as we know him, one God in three persons: Father, Son, and Holy Spirit.

Anyway, I had this self-righteous approach in judging my husband. Telling him that I knew what love was, and I walked in love toward him but that he did not walk in love toward me. Well, the next day I went to meet him after work to continue the argument, for intense fellowship, and to fight. While I was waiting for him in my car to get off from work, I had the audacity to begin reading 1 Corinthians 13:1–8, the "love chapter" as it is known. As I read, the Word of God, the Holy Spirit, began to convict me about my love walk. Reading down the list of the God kind of love, I could do nothing but repent and drive off. First Corinthians 13:5 tells us, "it does not dishonor others, it is not self-seeking, it is not easily angered and it keeps no record of wrong." Well, on that verse alone, I was busted right there on the spot. So I kindly packed up my Bible, drove home, fixed my family's dinner, and let the argument go because at that time, the Holy Spirit really convicted me. I was so bent on being right and not operate in God's love, which the righteousness of God leads us to do. Ever since that day of the Holy Spirit teaching me a lesson in love, the Word of God has spoken to me regarding God's love and dealing with me concerning my love walk. I realized that I had to cry out to God and ask him to teach me how to love. When we realize that we need help from God the Father, he is right there, ready and willing to assist us. So many people are able to help you but are not willing. God, however, is able and willing to help us in our love walks and anything else we may lay down before him at any time. Psalm 46:1 says that "God is our refuge and strength, an ever-present help in trouble." Are you willing and ready to obey what God has already instructed you to do, and that is walk in his love because he has poured out his love into our heart by the Holy Spirit?

Our ways seem right to us, but God wants us to learn his ways of doing things. Believe it or not, God is wiser and smarter than we are. His Word, the Bible, is filled with truth and direction for our lives, if we would just submit to its authority. If we are truly wise, we will come to understand we need to check in with the One who created us. Let the spirit of wisdom minister to you through reading the Word and in prayer. Most important, we need to stop examining ourselves against human standards and examine ourselves— our hearts and minds—through the Word of God: "He sent his word and healed them; he rescued them from the grave" (Psalm 107:20). So we need to examine ourselves and look through the mirror of God's Word.

God's help is available to assist us in our love walks, but we must be willing to cry out for help and ask him to teach us how to walk in his love, his way. The only way we are going to be able to walk in the God kind of love is by experience and example. The perfect example of God's love has been demonstrated for us through the personhood of Jesus Christ. While we were sinners and enemies of God, Christ died for us on the cross. Remember, practice makes perfect. Practice your love walk. The only way God is going to teach us how to walk in his love is through practice. Every day of your life you have a chance to practice how to walk in the God kind of love. Or are you going to continue to live and handle things like the natural person, the old person, your old self who does not want to ever give up. The sinner, the old person, will try to keep rising to the top and handle things. But you must be diligent in walking in the truth of God's love and his righteousness. The choice to love will always be ours.

The only way God is going to teach us how to love is by one experience at a time. Every day you and I are faced with opportunities to walk in the God kind of love or to walk in our own strengths, powers, and abilities. The only way we learn to love like God is if we decide and choose to love like him. We are called to walk in love. God, however, has not called us to be doormats for people to walk all over us and allow ourselves to be treated just any kind of way. As a child of God, we have the Holy Spirit and know when we are walking in love. Remember when we walk in God's love, we walk in God's power and his because greater is he who is in us than he who is in the world. "You, dear children, are from God and have overcome them, because the one who is in you is greater than the one who is in the world" (1 John 4:4).

God did not create us to be foolish people. A person who walks in the God kind of love is neither foolish nor pushovers. Because of the supernatural strength of God's love, we will be able to stand with power and authority in a hard place, deal with difficult people without being bitter or nasty, and continue to operate out of a place of power and authority.

Chapter 6

ANGER WITH NO RETALIATION

Ephesians 4:17–32
Hebrews 6:4–6
Romans 1:19–21; 8:26
Matthew 6:15; 18:35
Mark 4:25
1 Corinthians 10:13

The Word of God reminds us that we can be angry but to sin not. In other words, don't hold on to your anger, grudges, resentment, and bitterness no matter what. Don't act or react out of anger. Believe it or not, anger, a form of rage, is designed to destroy your life and the lives of those around you. If left unchecked, anger will fester and grow into other ill behaviors and attitudes such as hatefulness, bitterness, retaliation, and even murder. The Word of God says we ought to leave room for God's wrath. In Ephesians

4:26, the Word also says, "In your anger do not sin. Do not let the sun go down while you are still angry." When we operate out of ill spirits such as hatefulness and bitterness, we are not operating in the power and anointing of God. Nor are we living for his divine purpose when holding on to anger. The enemy tries to use anger to distract us, causing us to operate out of resentment, retaliation, and strife in the home, the workplace, and in the community.

Eventually, anger hatred, and any ill attitude will destroy you and others. A person cannot harbor unforgiveness, hostility, bitterness, and hatefulness in their hearts and minds and worship God or have a great prayer life. Think about it. What kind of witness for God would a person be if he or she operated out of a heart that was filled with hatefulness and bitterness? We ought to have righteousness, peace, and joy in the Holy Ghost with a pure heart. No one can carry righteousness, peace, and joy within their heart and at the same time have ill feelings within themselves.

Lay It Down

Mark 11:25 (AMP) tells us,

> Whenever you stand praying, if you have anything against anyone, forgive him [drop the issue, let it go], so that your Father who is in heaven will also forgive you your transgressions and wrongdoings [against Him and others]. [But if you do not forgive, neither will your Father in heaven forgive your transgressions.]

During difficult times, one cannot stand firm with illness in his or her heart and without the presence of God's peace. Daily we have to learn to lay things down—such as ill feelings, behaviors, and attitudes—at the foot of the cross. Let it go, whatever it is. Lay it all down in prayer at the foot of Jesus, at the foot of the cross. If you are holding something that does not edify your soul or glorify God the Father, lay it down. Let all bitterness, resentment, and unforgiveness go because they will bind up your spirit and block your blessings. When you feel as though you cannot make it and operate out of love and forgiveness, remember God is always a very present helper in trouble. He provides a way of escape out of anything.

We find in 1 Corinthians 10:13 (AMP),

> No temptation [regardless of its source] has overtaken or enticed you that is not common to human experience [nor is any temptation unusual or beyond human resistance]; but God is faithful [to His word—He is compassionate and trustworthy], and He will not let you be tempted beyond your ability [to resist], but along with the temptation He [has in the past and is now and] will [always] provide the way out as well, so that you will be able to endure it [without yielding, and will overcome temptation with joy.]

We cannot pay people back either as revenge and retaliation are not of God. You will hurt yourself trying to repay folk for hurting you. Don't waste your time and energy with retaliation. God also said revenge and vengeance are his, and he shall repay. Regarding retaliation, the enemy would like you to react in a manner unbecoming as a Christian in any given situation, so you will be a poor witness for Christ and not glorify God in your actions—especially during difficult times. The enemy wants you to embarrass or humiliate God and yourself by being a public disgrace. "It is impossible for those who have once been enlightened, who have tasted the heavenly gift, who have shared in the Holy Spirit, who have tasted the goodness of the word of God and the powers of the coming age and who have fallen away, to be brought back to repentance. To their loss they are crucifying the Son of God all over again and subjecting him" (Hebrews 6:4–6). But God the Father would have us to forgive each other because he first forgave us.

I'm convinced that the Word and the guidance of the Holy Spirit give us insight on forgiveness and anger. We are to display Christ like attitudes and godly characteristics. Once we have accepted God and Christ in our lives, it is our responsibility to grow spiritually. But one cannot grow spiritually and have an ill attitude and behavior. With resentment, bitterness, and anger resting in your spirit, you can't' have a good prayer life. It is hard to worship, honor, and glorify God while holding an ill attitude. It is impossible to live victoriously and serve God from a heart filled with strife, unforgiveness, and conflict. With all that illness in one's spirit, he or she would not be able to hear from God, thereby blocking blessings and divine spiritual growth.

The Holy Spirit Our Helper

The Holy Spirit and the Word of God are our helpers, God with us. And because God is with us, his presence is with us, so we can be committed while facing challenges in life and in difficult times. In his presence, we have fullness of joy. And in God's presence, we are empowered to overcome anything and everything. God said he will never leave or forsake us. God also made sure to give us his Word, which speaks to us. There are several scriptures I believe that speak to us, help us, guide us, and give us further understanding in the things of God. They will also help us to conduct ourselves in a godly manner in difficult and troubling times.

> In the same way the Spirit [comes to us and] helps us in our weakness. We do not know what prayer to offer or how to offer it as we should, but the Spirit Himself [knows our need and at the right time] intercedes on our behalf with sighs and groaning too deep for words. (Romans 8:26 AMP)

> So this I say, and solemnly affirm together with the Lord [as in His presence], that you must no longer live as the [unbelieving] Gentiles live, in the futility of their minds [and in the foolishness and emptiness of their souls], for their [moral] understanding is darkened and their reasoning is clouded; [they are] alienated and self-banished from the life of "God [with no share in it; this is] because of the [willful] ignorance and

spiritual blindness that is [deep-seated] within them, because of the hardness and insensitivity of their heart. And they, [the ungodly in their spiritual apathy], having become callous and unfeeling, have given themselves over [as prey] to unbridled sensuality, eagerly craving the practice of every kind of impurity [that their desires may demand]. But you did not learn Christ in this way! If in fact you have [really] heard Him and have been taught by Him, just as truth is in Jesus [revealed in His life and personified in Him], that, regarding your previous way of life, you put off your old self [completely discard your former nature], which is being corrupted through deceitful desires, and be continually renewed in the spirit of your mind [having a fresh, untarnished mental and spiritual attitude], and put on the new self [the regenerated and renewed nature], created in God's image, [godlike] in the righteousness and holiness of the truth [living in a way that expresses to God your gratitude for your salvation].

Therefore, rejecting all falsehood [whether lying, defrauding, telling half-truths, spreading rumors, any such as these], speak truth each one with his neighbor, for we are all parts of one another [and we are all parts of the body of Christ]. Be angry [at sin—at immorality, at injustice, at ungodly behavior], yet do not sin; do not let your anger [cause you shame, nor allow it to] last until the sun goes down. And do not give the devil an opportunity [to lead you into sin by holding a grudge, or nurturing anger, or harboring resentment, or cultivating bitterness]. The thief [who has become a believer] must no longer steal, but instead he must work hard [making an honest living], producing that which is good with his own hands, so that he will have something to share with those in need. Do not let unwholesome [foul, profane, worthless, vulgar] words ever come out of your mouth, but only such speech as is good for building up others, according to the need and the occasion, so that it will be a blessing to those who hear [you speak]. And do not grieve the Holy Spirit of God [but seek to please Him], by whom you were sealed and marked [branded as God's own] for the day of redemption [the final deliverance from the consequences of sin]. Let all bitterness and wrath and anger and clamor [perpetual animosity, resentment, and strife, fault-finding] and slander be put away from you, along with every kind of malice [all spitefulness, verbal abuse, malevolence]. Be kind and helpful to one another, tender-hearted [compassionate, understanding], forgiving one another [readily and freely], just as God in Christ also forgave you. (Ephesians 4:17-32 AMP)

I believe we gain power and strength through the act of forgiveness. Forgiveness is a very powerful act of love. Jesus operated in the act of forgiveness all the time. He was so full of the love of the Father that he refused to hurt those who hurt and tried to destroy him. In Luke 23:34, Jesus said, "Father, forgive them; for they do not know what they are doing."

But if you do not forgive others [nurturing your hurt and anger with the result that it interferes with your relationship with God], then your Father will not forgive your trespasses. (Matthew 6:15 AMP)

Because that which is known about God is evident within them [in their inner consciousness], for God made it evident to them; for ever since the creation of the world His invisible attributes, His eternal power and divine nature, have been clearly seen, being understood through His workmanship [all His creation, the wonderful things that He has made], so that they [who fail to believe and trust in Him] are without excuse and without defense. For even though they knew God [as the Creator], they did not honor Him as God or give thanks [for His wondrous creation]. On the contrary, they became worthless in their thinking [godless, with pointless reasoning's, and silly speculations], and their foolish heart was darkened. (Romans 1:19–21 AMP)

Chapter 7

OUT OF REVERENCE FOR THE FATHER

Being subject to one another out of reverence for Christ,

—Ephesians 5:21 (AMP)

1 Samuel 16–20
Luke 23:34
Ephesians 4:23; 5:15–21
Matthew 5:43–48
John 1:14
Romans 12:2, 19
Acts 9
James 1:7
Philippians 2:5, 12; 4:8
Hebrews 12:1
John 15:1

Mark 11:25

2 Corinthians 10:5–7

Colossians 3:2–3, 10

Learn to Forgive Out of Reverence for God

1 Samuel 16–20

> But the Lord said to Samuel, "Do not look at his appearance or at the height of his stature, because I have rejected him. For the Lord sees not as man sees; for man looks at the outward appearance, but the Lord looks at the heart." Then Jesse called Abinadab and had him pass before Samuel. But Samuel said, "The Lord has not chosen this one either." Next Jesse had Shammah pass by. And Samuel said, "The Lord has not chosen him either." Jesse had seven of his sons pass before Samuel. But Samuel said to Jesse, "The Lord has not chosen [any of] these." Then Samuel said to Jesse, "Are all your sons here?" Jesse replied, "There is still one left, the youngest; he is tending the sheep." Samuel said to Jesse, "Send word and bring him; because we will not sit down [to eat the sacrificial meal] until he comes here, (1 Samuel 16:7–11 AMP).

In 1 Samuel 16:1–23, God sent the prophet Samuel to anoint one of Jesse's sons. Jesse, David's father, had seven sons. But his father did not even remember him until after the prophet Samuel looked at all of David's brothers and said that it was none of them, that God sent him to anoint another. Jesse then remembered he had another son, David. David was a little shepherd boy, Jesse's youngest son. David would be a giant slayer, lion killer, and one who would one day become king. David had to learn the power of forgiveness while he was committed in a difficult place. After David was anointed by the prophet Samuel to do the special work of the Lord, he was constantly faced with dealing with difficult people as he became the mighty man of God. Although David's father and brothers, especially Eliab, saw him as a "shepherd boy," King David remained confident in whom God made and saw him.

Once David was anointed by Samuel, he began to speak and act with authority. David began to step into the role, the office of where God was calling him to, to be King. He had to deal with major jealousy from people who were supposed to be close to him. Not only was King Saul jealous of David, his big brother Eliab was especially angry and jealous toward him for no reason at all. He spoke negatively toward David as David delivered food to the soldiers' camp as he was instructed to do so. Eliab accused David of becoming proud and wicked, but David remained in agreement and confident in whom God said he was. Eliab would later come around and support his little brother even as he became King David.

One day as David was delivering food to the soldiers, Eliab asked him what he was doing there. Eliab then said to him that he should not be there because he was not a proper soldier. David ignored his big brother and continued serving food and encouraging the solders, reminding them that God was on their side. Eliab said in a demeaning way to David, "Who did you leave them few sheep with?" At that point, David ignored his brother, forgave him, and kept doing what needed to be done.

King David also understood that when we try to destroy and hurt people, we are operating against God the Father. David was under the power of the Holy Spirit, which helped him keep his heart right with God. There was another time in which David encountered another jealous yet powerful and difficult man who was in authority—King Saul.

> So David went out wherever Saul sent him, and he acted wisely and prospered; and Saul appointed him over the men of war. And it pleased all the people and also Saul's servants. As they were coming [home], when David returned from killing the Philistine, the women came out of all the cities of Israel, singing and dancing, to meet King Saul with tambourines, [songs of] joy, and musical instruments. The women sang as they played and danced, saying, "Saul has slain his thousands, And David his ten thousands." Then Saul became very angry, for this saying displeased him; and he said, "They have ascribed to David ten thousands, but to me they have ascribed [only] thousands. Now what more can he have but the kingdom?" Saul looked at David with suspicion [and jealously] from that day forward. (1 Samuel 18:5–9 AMP)

David served King Saul as a sacred musician, warrior, and trusted servant. But King Saul then became enraged and jealous of David's gifts and skills. But David did not retaliate or try to kill King Saul even when he could. David understood the power and authority of having reverence for God the Father and not to operate in revenge, animosity, jealousy, or strife. Rather, to act with love, trust, respect, and honor for people out of reverence for God the Father even when being in a tight, difficult place and dealing with difficult people.

Jonathan, King David's friend, was also in a difficult position of being a friend with a person his dad disliked. We all can relate to that type of position. Have you ever had a friend whom you adored and loved, but your parents or other friends did not care for the person? Well, so was the case of Jonathan, King Saul, and King David. This was an awkward situation for David to be in because King Saul had helped make David king. Not only did David have to deal with King Saul as a difficult person in authority, but his beloved friend Jonathan also had to deal with his father, King Saul, a complex, complicated, and difficult person. Because Jonathan greatly cared for David, he found himself in a hard place and a difficult time. Jonathan loved, respected, and obeyed his father, but King Saul continued to admit openly that he was going to pursue David and kill him, although he promised Jonathan he would not.

King Saul grew more and more jealous of David's success because people admired him as a great warrior and an anointed man of God. So it became very difficult for Jonathan to remain committed to both his father and his friend. Jonathan loved and honored his father, even though he was wrong in his pursuit of David to kill him. Jonathan took a great liking to David, who he grew to appreciate and love like a brother. The covenant that Jonathan made with David stopped him from obeying his father's orders to kill David. Though Jonathan was put in a difficult situation, he found a way to be committed to the people he greatly loved. Jonathan had to be committed in a hard, difficult place.

Out of Reverence for God, Learn to Love and Honor

Nabal and Abigail: 1 Samuel 25

> Therefore see that you walk carefully [living life with honor, purpose, and courage; shunning those who tolerate and enable evil], not as the unwise, but as wise [sensible, intelligent, discerning people], making the very most of your time [on earth, recognizing and taking advantage of each opportunity and using it with wisdom and diligence], because the days are [filled with] evil. Therefore do not be foolish and thoughtless, but understand and firmly grasp what the will of the Lord is. Do not get drunk with wine, for that is wickedness (corruption, stupidity), but be filled with the [Holy] Spirit and constantly guided by Him. Speak to one another in psalms and hymns and spiritual songs, [offering praise by] singing and making melody with your heart to the Lord; always giving thanks to

God the Father for all things, in the name
of our Lord Jesus Christ; being subject to
one another out of reverence for Christ.
(Ephesians 5:15–21 AMP)

Abigail, a loving, beautiful, mighty woman of God, had grace, strength, intelligence, wisdom, and kindness. She loved and honored a difficult person, her husband Nabal. Although Nabal was not a loving and honorable man, Abigail honored and respected him in his position anyway. She looked past her husband's offensive, rude characteristics and honored him in spite of his shortcomings. Sometimes out of our reverence for God, we have to look past people's rude, harsh, offensive attitudes and characteristics and love the evil wickedness out of them.

Not much is known of this extraordinary woman, except Abigail was married to a difficult man. Nabal was known to be harsh and evil, especially in his businesses dealings as a shepherd and goat herder. Yet Abigail acted nobly toward him when he was not such a nice person. Just like Abigail, sometimes we have to be committed in making a difference for the better, even when we're uncomfortable dealing with difficult people.

Abigail was also known for exercising great wisdom in how she maneuvered, acted, and reacted toward David during his years on the run from the jealous King Saul. In 1 Samuel 25, we see Abigail move in wisdom on behalf of Nabal during a time when his flock of sheep and goats were in danger of being stolen while posturing at a nearby camp where David's men were attending their flock. A band of Ishmaelite thieves were roaming the wilderness, stealing and causing harm to un-expecting herdsmen in the area. David and his men were noblemen, men of courage, who protected Nabal's men from the band of thieves and crooks as caring neighbors. After helping Nabal's men, David sent some of his men to request some form of recognition, appreciation, or compensation for their efforts. However, Nabal refused them, mocked them, ridiculed them, and even insulted them. As the foolish person Nabal was known to be, and before word got back to David of Nabal's foolish behavior and mockery of them, Abigail stepped in with a kind gesture.

Soon after David got word of Nabal's mockery, David told his men to suit up with their armor and their swords because they were going to pursue Nabal and show him that if it were not for them protecting him, he would not have prospered in his business. Well, thank God word got back to Abigail first about what was about to happened. Abigail, through Nabal's servant, found out what was going on between her husband and David. So Abigail sent Nabal's servant to meet David and apologize for her husband's bad behavior. Meanwhile, David informed his men to prepare for battle. But because Abigail was informed by Nabal's servant of what was happening, she was able to stop the major conflict between her husband and David.

> But David's men were very good to us, and we were not harmed or treated badly, nor did we miss anything as long as we were with them, when we were in the fields. They were a wall [of protection] to us both night and day, all the time that we were

with them tending the sheep. Now then, know this and consider what you should do, for evil is [already] planned against our master and against all his household; but he is such a worthless and wicked man that one cannot speak [reasonably] to him. (1 Samuel 25:15–17 AMP)

Abigail Intercedes: 1 Samuel 25:18–38 (AMP)

Then Abigail hurried and took two hundred loaves of bread, two jugs of wine, five sheep already prepared [for roasting], five measures of roasted grain, a hundred clusters of raisins, and two hundred cakes of figs, and loaded them on donkeys. She said to her young men (servants), "Go on ahead of me; behold, I am coming after you." But she did not tell her husband Nabal. (1 Samuel 25:18–19 AMP)

Kneeling at his feet she said, "My lord, let the blame and guilt be on me alone. And please let your maidservant speak to you, and listen to the words of your maidservant. Please do not let my lord pay attention to this worthless man," Nabal, for as his name is, so is he. Nabal (fool) is his name and foolishness (stupidity) is with him; but I your maidservant did not see my lord's young men whom you sent. (1 Samuel 25:24–25 AMP)

Please forgive the transgression of your maidservant; for the Lord will certainly make my lord a secure and enduring house, because my lord is fighting the battles of the LORD, and evil will not be found in you all your days. Should anyone rise up to pursue you and to seek your life, then the life of my lord will be bound in the [precious] bundle of the living with the Lord your God; but the lives of your enemies—those He will hurl out as from the center of a sling. (1 Samuel 25:28–29 AMP)

David said to Abigail, "Blessed be the Lord, the God of Israel, who sent you to meet me this day. And blessed be your discretion and discernment, and blessed be you, who has kept me from bloodshed this day and from avenging myself by my own hand. Nevertheless, as the Lord the God of Israel lives, who has prevented me from harming you, if you had not come quickly to meet me, most certainly by the morning light there would not have been left to Nabal so much as one male." So David accepted what she had brought to him and said to her, "Go up to your house in peace. See, I have listened to you and have granted your request." Then Abigail came to Nabal, and he was holding a feast in his house [for the shearers], like the feast of a king.

And Nabal's mood was joyous because he was very drunk; so she told him nothing at all until the morning light. But in the morning, when Nabal was sober, and his wife told him these things, his heart died within him and he became [paralyzed and helpless] like a stone. About ten days later Nabal died. (1 Samuel 25:32–38 AMP)

David Marries Abigail: 1 Samuel 25:39–42 (AMP)

When David heard that Nabal was dead, he said, blessed be the Lord, who has pleaded the cause of my reproach [suffered] at the hand of Nabal and has kept His servant from [retaliating with] evil. For the Lord has returned the wickedness of Nabal on his own head." Then David sent word to Abigail, proposing to take her as his wife. When the servants of David came to Abigail at Carmel, they said to her, "David sent us to you to take you [to him] to be his wife." And she stood and bowed with her face to the ground and said, "Behold, your maidservant is [ready to be] a maid to wash the feet of the servants of my lord." Then Abigail quickly got up, and rode on a donkey, with five of her maidens who attended her; and she followed the messengers of David and became his wife.

David understood that when we destroy and hurt people, we are working against God the Father. Basically, when we hurt people, we hurt God for it is God's desire that we love each other and are kind and caring for each other, especially during difficult times. I contend that some people, even some Christian brothers and sisters, don't realize or understand that when they mistreat people, they will one day give an account to God for how they handled people. How can we claim to love God, whom we have never seen, and not love people we see every day? "We love because he first loved us. Whoever claims to love God yet hates a brother or sister is a liar. For whoever does not love their brother and sister, whom they have seen, cannot love God, whom they have not seen" (1 John 4:19–20). Even Saul, who became Paul, one of the main Disciples of Christ, came to understand and learn this fact: We should not mistreat people. Before Paul's conversion and becoming a Christ follower and a disciple, he killed believers. One day God confronted Paul, who was on his way to kill Christians by way of Straight Street. God asked him in Acts 9:4, "he fell to the ground and heard a voice say to him, "Saul, Saul, why do you persecute me?"" Believe it not we will give an account and answer to God for how we conduct ourselves and treat people. After Paul's conversion and his encounter with a loving, forgiving God, Paul became one of God's major champions of the New Testament by writing, preaching, and teaching more than half of the New Testament. Now it is awesome how God tuned Paul's life totally around.

Paul, however, first accepted the forgiveness of God and then he had to forgive himself. After Paul acknowledged and accepted God's forgiveness, he accepted Jesus Christ as Lord and the love of God. Finally, Paul learned to love others as he loved himself. With Paul's past of being a monster and murderer of God's people, I'm sure he had to face lots of challenging times and hard places in his life. Because Paul grew spiritually, he was able to accomplish major milestones in his life. Paul was able to be committed to the call and purpose of God on his life, even while being in a hard place. Throughout the New Testament, it is been recorded how God used Paul to be committed in a difficult times. Paul stated in Philippians 4:12–14 (AMP):

> I know how to get along and live humbly [in difficult times], and I also know how to enjoy abundance and live in prosperity. In any and every circumstance I have learned the secret [of facing life], whether well-fed or going hungry, whether having an abundance or being in need. I can do all things [which He has called me to do] through Him who strengthens and empowers me [to fulfill His purpose—I am self-sufficient in Christ's sufficiency; I am ready for anything and equal to anything through Him who infuses me with inner strength and confident peace.] Nevertheless, it was right of you to share [with me] in my difficulties.

Saul's Conversion: *Acts 9:1–19 (NIV)*

> Meanwhile, Saul was still breathing out murderous threats against the Lord's

disciples. He went to the high priest and asked him for letters to the synagogues in Damascus, so that if he found any there who belonged to the Way, whether men or women, he might take them as prisoners to Jerusalem. As he neared Damascus on his journey, suddenly a light from heaven flashed around him. He fell to the ground and heard a voice say to him, "Saul, Saul, why do you persecute me?" "Who are you, Lord?" Saul asked. "I am Jesus, whom you are persecuting," he replied.

Don't Be a Spiritual Schizophrenic

Schizophrenia is a long-term mental disorder involving a breakdown in the relationship between thought, emotion, and behavior. This leads to faulty perceptions, inappropriate actions and feelings, withdrawal from reality and personal relationships into fantasies and delusions, and a sense of mental fragmentation.

In the natural sometimes when someone may be diagnosed and suffered from a psychological disorder. One such diagnosis when something is mentally wrong is sometimes known as schizophrenia; which is a disorder of someone who may be undeveloped mentally. So with this disorder, in the natural world, doctors prescribe medication to treat the condition. Since we are Christians, we should not remain spiritually immature, someone with a double mindset. James 1:7 tells us that a double-minded person is unstable in all his or her ways and should not expect anything from the Lord. As Christians we must demonstrate and exemplify the attributes, the mindset of Christ, which are love, joy, peace, and forgiveness. The enemy knows that if he can get you to operate in things like unforgiveness, holding grudges, the spirit of being offended, resentment, revenge, vengeance, retaliation, and any sort of ill feelings or mindset, you will not live a blessed life. The enemy is comes to kill, steal, and destroy your life. He wants to hinder, block, or even stop your blessings, break through and stop your spiritual progress. If ill feelings are left unchecked and you give yourself over to them, they are left to fester. Ill feelings, an ill mindset, are like poisoning yourself and dying a slow death from within. Unfortunately, we are in a battle for our minds. God's Word speaks a lot about our spiritual mindsets. I believe a healthy spiritual mindset will glorify God in the spiritual and natural realms. Isaiah 26:3 (AMP) says, "you will keep in perfect and constant peace the one whose mind is steadfast [that is, committed and focused on you-in both inclination and character], because he trusts and takes refuge in you [with hope and confident expectation]." The Word of God also reminds us in Romans 12:2 (AMP), "And do not be conformed to this world [any longer with its superficial values and customs], but be transformed and progressively changed [as you mature spiritually] by the renewing of your mind [focusing on godly values and ethical attitudes], so that you may prove [for yourselves] what the will of God is, that which is good and acceptable and perfect [in His plan and purpose for you]." Also, in Ephesians 4:23–24 (AMP), "and be continually renewed in the spirit of your mind [having a fresh, untarnished mental and spiritual attitude], and put on the new self [the regenerated and renewed nature], created in God's image, [godlike] in the righteousness and holiness of the truth [living in a way that expresses to God your gratitude for your salvation]." Finally, Jesus came demonstrating and teaching us how to live in the earthly realm. He was the Word that became flesh and lived among us. "And the Word (Christ) became flesh, and lived among us; and we [actually] saw His glory, glory as belongs to the [One and] only begotten Son of the Father, [the Son who is truly unique, the only One of His kind, who is] full of grace and truth (absolutely free of deception)" (John 1:14 AMP).

Jesus said that the enemy comes to kill steal and destroy our lives. If our mindsets are not healthy, our lives will be off course, and the enemy knows that. So the enemy comes with ideas, thoughts, and suggestions to distract, stop, hinder, block, and destroy our lives by any means necessary. So often through an unhealthy mindset, one's life is destroyed. As God's people, we must remember that apart from God, we can do nothing. So when the enemy comes after your mindset in any way, you can go forth in your purpose knowing that God the Father is with you. And because you know God is with you and for you, meditate on his Word because we were created to operate through a godly mindset. That is why Jesus had the strength to operate with such power and authority, even when things got rough; he operated from a godly mindset. Jesus had such power to forgive and be committed in a hard place simply out of having the right mindset.

Right before Jesus died on the cross, he looked toward the heavens and asked God the Father to forgive the people who were killing him. Jesus demonstrated for us the ultimate power of forgiveness: and Jesus was saying, "Father, forgive them; for they do not know what they are doing" (Luke 23:34 AMP). They cast lots, dividing his clothes among themselves. Mark 11:25 (AMP) reminds us that we should always forgive as we were forgiven: "Whenever you stand praying, if you have anything against anyone, forgive him [drop the issue, let it go], so that your Father who is in heaven will also forgive you your transgressions and wrongdoings [against Him and others]." He knew that if we are going to be victorious in our purposes in this life, we must operate out of a clean, clear, pure heart, consciousness, and mindset if we are going to be in accord with God and the Holy Spirit. King David did, just as Jesus did; they worshipped and served God the Father of pure hearts and godly mindsets.

King David also understood that one cannot worship God the Father out of a heart and mind filled with ill feelings like unforgiveness, bitterness, and strife. King David asked God to create in him a clean heart and renew a right spirit within him because he knew, just like Jesus knew, that he could not have victory over the cross, death, burial, and the grave unless he had a pure heart and mindset. Jesus had to triumph in the resurrection and ultimately be seated on the right side of God the Father.

Jesus continuously reminded everyone what he had encountered and that he was about his Father's business. Jesus knew that one cannot operate in love and unforgiveness at the same time. Since he was God with us, Immanuel, he had to demonstrate love since he was love. Jesus had too much to accomplish to operate in unforgiveness. He knew he had to stay focused. He could not have a double mind. It was no time to operate out of a schizophrenic mindset.

Jesus knew that he had strength, supernatural strength in forgiveness. He knew that he needed super natural power to move to the next level. Jesus also knew that unforgiveness was poisonous, and the will destroy you if left to fester and grow into bitterness, revenge, resentment, retaliation, hatefulness, pain, anger, and unresolved issues in the mind.

Jesus stayed focused on what his Father called him to do. And he had sense enough to know that you cannot move in two directions at the same time; you can't be in the things of God and a devil at the same time. You can't go up and down, left and right, love and hate all at the same time. Jesus knew that right thinking causes right action. He knew we should think on things that are pure, good, and of praise that would give him the right mindset: "Finally, brothers and sisters, whatever is true, whatever is noble, whatever is right, whatever is pure, whatever is lovely, whatever is admirable—if anything is excellent or praiseworthy—think about such things" (Philippians 4:8). This is why the Word tells us to cast down vain imagination and everything that tries to exalt itself above the knowledge of God, the knowledge that we know God to be a good Father and a loving and forgiving God. Second Corinthians 10:5–7 tells us, "We demolish arguments and every pretension that sets itself up against the knowledge of God, and we take captive every thought to make it obedient to Christ. And we will be ready to punish every act of disobedience, once your obedience is complete. You are judging by appearances. If anyone is confident that they belong to Christ, they should consider again that we belong to Christ just as much as they do." While we were yet sinners, Christ died for us in love and forgiveness. Jesus knew that vengeance belonged to

God: "Beloved, never avenge yourselves, but leave the way open for God's wrath [and His judicial righteousness]; for it is written [in Scripture], 'Vengeance is Mine, I will repay,' says the Lord" (Romans 12:19 AMP). He knew that we should not do evil for evil but overcome evil with good. In the book of James, the Word also says where there is envy, jealousy, and strife, there is confusion, and every evil work is present.

You cannot have two mindsets at the same time and have peace in your heart with God. Jesus was able to be committed in a hard place because he was focused on the Father and what he had come to do. Although Jesus was not living in heaven at the time, he had set his mind on things above, not on earthly things. We can't live life with our heads up in the clouds, but we can choose to have a godly mindset and to be kind, loving, and operate out of peace toward all people. It is important for us to put to death our former negative, defeated lives and mindsets, and put our minds and hearts on things above, on the new person, new self by being renewed in our knowledge of him, our Father, our Creator. Colossians 3:2–3, 10 (AMP) tells us, "Set your mind and keep focused habitually on the things above [the heavenly things], not on things that are on the earth [which have only temporal value]. For you died [to this world], and your [new, real] life is hidden with Christ in God. ... And have put on the new [spiritual] self who is being continually renewed in true knowledge in the image of Him who created the new self."

The enemy is continuously trying to make people leave their assignments from God. And if he can't get you to leave your assignments, he will try to distract you, if not distract, he will try to block or hinder you from being that man or woman on God's assignment, on God's divine plan for your life. We must be determined not to give up or give in on your set place. Worship God no matter what. Stay committed to God and his call and purpose in life, no matter what. We have to trust God, no matter what. Even King David said, "When my Father and my mother forsake me the Lord will left me up." We must not care who or what may come against us; we have to trust the Lord God Almighty, who always causes us to triumph and make a way for us in a difficult place. Let us not lose heart in doing good, for in due time, we will reap if we do not grow weary, faint, and give up in your difficult time. "Let us not grow weary or become discouraged in doing good, for at the proper time we will reap, if we do not give in" (Galatians 6:9 AMP).

Chapter 8

SUFFERED BUT BLESSED, PROSPEROUS

The Lord is close to the brokenhearted and saves those who are crushed in spirit.

—Psalm 34:18

Genesis 34; 37:311; 39:2, 23, 40; 41:45, 50–52; 50:19–20;
Job 1:1–12, 20–22; 13:15–16; 2:9–10; 22:21; 42:10–12
Mark 9:23–25
Romans 8:28–31
Philippians 4:11–13
Galatians 5:14, 22
Psalm 34:18

Prospering through Struggling

When we think of people during biblical times that had tremendous losses and much pain, rejection, and setbacks, we often think of Joseph and Job. Joseph and Job had a lot of hurt during their lives. They suffered many difficulties while being committed in a hard place. When we think of these two men in regards to suffering, they both were committed to others as well us to God the Father in the midst of their suffering. They both still prospered regardless of their suffering, and they persevered in their faith. These two men are perfect examples of great prosperity but not in the absence of much suffering. I believe they were so blessed and prosperous even the more because of their commitments to God and their kindness and compassion for others during a difficult time. Both were tested through and through. But these men kept their integrity. Joseph and Job had a sense that God was with them and loved and cared for them although they suffered greatly. There are two scriptures that come to mind. Each man spoke while in his suffering and when coming out of his suffering. The scriptures following tell me that they were reassured of God's commitment to them in spite of what they were going through.

I. One of the first persons to come to mind who remained committed amid struggling was Joseph. In all that he went through, God showed himself to be mighty and faithful in Joseph's restoration. In Genesis 50:19–20 (AMP), Joseph responded beautifully to his brothers, who caused most of the difficulties in his life by mistreating him.

> But Joseph said to them, do not be afraid,
> for am I in the place of God? [Vengeance
> is His, not mine.] As for you, what you
> meant evil against me, but God meant it
> for good in order to bring about this present
> outcome, that many people would be kept
> alive [as they are this day].

As Joseph help shepherd his family's flock, his brothers plotted to kill him because they felt as though their father, Jacob, favored and loved Joseph so much more than them. Jacob made Joseph a special coat, a tunic of many colors, which was very costly. One day when Joseph was separated from his brothers while looking after the flock, they plotted to kill him. As Joseph returned to his brothers, they said among themselves, "The dreamer cometh." Earlier, Joseph may have seemed a little braggadocio with them as he shared a dream of one day ruling over them. Joseph's brothers quickly grew to despise him and became very jealous of him.

God loved Joseph and trusted his heart. Remember, God looks at our hearts. So God visited Joseph in a series of several dreams, giving him a glimpse into the window of his future, a very prosperous future. Not fully mature in the things of God and the spiritual realm, Joseph shared the dreams with his very jealous and envious brothers. God, however, could trust Joseph with pain, hurt, and mistreatment because he knew Joseph would not retaliate in any way toward his brothers for treating him badly. He also knew that once Joseph entered into power, he would not misuse his authority and abuse those who had hurt him in the past. Joseph's brothers felt as if Joseph was proud, and they hated him even the more and desired to kill him. But instead, they sold their brother into slavery with a band of Ishmaelites, who were wandering traders.

As time moved on, Jacob mourned what he believed was the death of his beloved son. Meanwhile, Joseph was living in Egypt as a slave with one setback, disappointment and difficulties one right after the other. Yet Joseph continued in his faithfulness in service.

> Now Israel (Jacob) loved Joseph more than all his children, because he was the son of his old age; and he made him a [distinctive] multicolored tunic. His brothers saw that their father loved Joseph more than all of his brothers; so they hated him and could not [find it within themselves to] speak to him on friendly terms. Now Joseph dreamed a dream, and he told it to his brothers, and they hated him even more. He said to them, "Please listen to [the details of] this dream which I have dreamed; we [brothers] were binding sheaves [of grain stalks] in the field, and lo, my sheaf [suddenly] got up and stood upright and remained standing; and behold, your sheaves stood all around my sheaf and bowed down [in respect]." His brothers said to him, "Are you actually going to reign over us? Are you really going to rule and govern us as your subjects?" So they hated him even more for [telling them about] his dreams and for his [arrogant]

words. But Joseph dreamed still another dream, and told it to his brothers [as well]. He said, "See here, I have again dreamed a dream, and lo, [this time I saw] eleven stars and the sun and the moon bowed down [in respect] to me!" He told it to his father as well as to his brothers; but his father rebuked him and said to him [in disbelief], "What is [the meaning of] this dream that you have dreamed? Shall I and your mother and your brothers actually come to bow down to the ground [in respect] before you?" Joseph's brothers were envious and jealous of him, but his father kept the words [of Joseph] in mind [wondering about their meaning]. (Genesis 37:3–11 AMP)

Joseph was sold into slavery once again by the Midianites to Potiphar, captain of the royal guard. Genesis 39:2 (AMP) tells us, "The Lord was with Joseph, [even though a slave] became a successful and prosperous man; everything Joseph put his hands to, it was blessed." Joseph was a trustworthy person, so Potiphar left all that he owned in Joseph's hand. But while Potiphar was away on business, his wife found Joseph to be handsome and attractive. Still a mighty man of God with integrity, Joseph did not give in to her advances. The evilness of Potiphar's wife caused her to lie about Joseph, accusing him of trying to lie with her. The warden where Joseph went to prison for supposedly abusing Potiphar's wife favored Joseph because the Lord was with him. Even in prison, Joseph prospered. He still ministered love, kindness, and compassion to those around him, even in the face of difficulties himself. Why, because he was committed to God. He knew that although in prison, God was still committed to and with him. He helped the chief cupbearer and the chief baker with interpretations of their dreams. Their meanings came to pass, just as Joseph said they would.

After word got out and began to spread that God was with Joseph and his spiritual insight and gifts, he was released from prison to Pharaoh. Joseph stood before Pharaoh, who acknowledged that there was none other like Joseph in all the land, and that Joseph had the divine Spirit of God dwelling in him. Because of Joseph's faithfulness, compassion, and kindness in the prison, he was in the palace before Pharaoh. Joseph was committed to God even in a hard and difficult place, Potipher's house and the prison. When things went from bad to worse, Joseph remained committed. Joseph was in the place God promised and showed him in dreams when he was a teenager; the place that he shared with his jealous, envious brothers of where he would be one day. He had become royalty, a mighty man of God, and second in command and power to Pharaoh.

After Joseph was put in place, Pharaoh said in Genesis 40:44 (AMP), "though I'am Pharaoh, yet without your permission shall no man raise his hand [to do anything] or set his foot [to go anywhere] in all the land of Egypt [all classes of people submit to your authority]." Then Pharaoh named him Joseph "Zaphenath–paneah," meaning Hebrew, and gave him Asenath, the daughter of Potiphera, priest of Helioplish in Egypt as his wife. "Asenath" means misfortune and some say she was born out of rape. However, in some rabbinical literature, it is believed that Asenath was actually the daughter of Joseph's sister Dinah. This would mean that Asenath was Joseph's niece.

Dinah was believed to have been raped when she was taken by one of the men from the Shechemite community, who wanted to intermarry with Jacob's tribe. But Jacob's sons were not having it, Simeon and Levi, especially. Shechem, the son of Hamor the Hivitye, the prince of the land, saw her and took her. He laid with her, and he humbled her." Some suggest that the intercourse he had with her was consensual; others suggest it was rape. Nevertheless, Dinah's brothers—Jacob's sons by his first wife, Leah—were not having any of it either way, consensual or otherwise.

Some teachings suggest that Asenath was taken by angels to the land of Egypt, where she was adopted by Potiphera. Some versions of the story further suggest that she was identified by a special plate around her neck, placed by Jacob, that bore the name of God and the story of her conception. It has also been believed that Asenath was killed as an infant, lest it be said that there was harlotry in the tent of Jacob instead of Jacob, her grandfather, hanging a gold plate around her neck and sending her away.

Other teachings supposedly say that God sent the archangel Michael to bring Asenath to the house of an Egyptian. A servant found her crying near the home of Potiphera. When Potiphera saw the plate around Asenath's neck, he said, "This is the daughter of the great one." This narrative teaches that God orchestrated this so Joseph would have a suitable wife.

Joseph, a Hebrew name meaning he will add and the name Pharaoh gave Joseph, Zaphenath–paneah, which means one who discovers hidden things, have not only great significance, but the two sons he had by Asenath has significant names as well. In Genesis 41:51–52 (AMP) we find, "Joseph named the firstborn Manasseh (causing to forget), for he said, 'God has made me forget all my trouble and hardship and all [the sorrow of the loss of] my father's household.' He named the second [son] Ephraim (fruitfulness), for 'God has caused me to be fruitful and very successful in the land of my suffering.'" In other words, God the Father can cause you to be successful right in the place where you had your greatest pain and struggles. This is so awesome. God can take what was meant to hurt and destroy you and turn it around to bless you and give him glory. "And we know [with great confidence] that God [who is deeply concerned about us] causes all things to work together [as a plan] for good for those who love God, to those who are called according to His plan and purpose" (Romans 8:28 AMP).

Restoration: Better than Before

Job was the second man who suffered great loss and many difficulties, yet God was committed to him, and he remained committed to God. God had even spoken well of Job:

> there was a man in the land of Uz whose name was Job; he was a blameless and upright man of many great qualities. This man Job was one who feared God [with reverence; he abstained and turned away from evil [because he honored God]. Seven sons and

three daughters were born to him. He also possessed 7,000 sheep, 3,000 camels, 500 yoke (pairs) of oxen, 500 female donkeys, and a very great number of servants, so that this man was the greatest [and wealthiest and most respected] of all the men of the east (northern Arabia). (Job1:1–3 AMP)

Job's Character and Wealth

We find in Job 1:6–12 (AMP),

Now there was a day when the sons of God (angels) came to present themselves before the Lord, and Satan (adversary, accuser) also came among them. The Lord said to Satan, "From where have you come?" Then Satan answered the Lord, "From roaming around on the earth and from walking around on it." The LORD said to Satan, "Have you considered and reflected on My servant Job? For there is none like him on the earth, a blameless and upright man, one who fears God [with reverence] and abstains from and turns away from evil [because he honors God]." Then Satan answered the Lord, "Does Job fear God for nothing? Have You not put a hedge [of protection] around him and his house and all that he has, on every side? You have blessed the work of his hands [and conferred prosperity and happiness upon him], and his possessions have increased in the land. But put forth Your hand now and touch (destroy) all that he has, and he will surely curse You to Your face." Then the Lord said to Satan, Behold, all that Job has is in your power, only do not put your hand on the man himself." So Satan departed from the presence of the Lord.

Now if God the Father acknowledges you as being a good person who is upright and blameless, yet he knows all about you, including your faults and weaknesses but still choose to be committed to you, what can anyone else have to say concerning you? Nothing. How awesome is that to have the Creator acknowledge you and his love for you in spite of and regardless of what is said, thought, or believed about you or any downfalls you may have experienced. "What, then, shall we say in response to these things? If God be for us, who can be against us" (Romans 8:31). Now that is commitment; that's unconditional love. Job knew that God was committed to him and was for him.

While Job and his family were going about their daily lives, God and Satan had a unique conversation regarding Job. And because Job was a person of integrity, God bragged about Job being an upright man and a good person. Out of the unique conversation, Satan requested and was then allowed to test Job's commitment to God, but he was not allowed to harm him. One day messengers—one right after another—came to Job with bad news regarding the sudden deaths of all his children; he had seven sons and three daughters. Being one of the greatest men of the east, Job lost it all. The test, Satan's attack of Job had begun. Job lost everything and all his children and servants, except for the servant who reported what happened and his wife. He had great loss of his possessions, including all his sheep, camels, yoke of oxen, and donkeys.

The presence of a trusting God, I believe, is not about the absence of trouble and things falling apart. Rather, in the face of trouble and difficulty, we have an opportunity to use our faith. I believe that Job knew God had a purpose for his troubles and pain. Soon after Job's great loss, he trusted God that much more. He remained so committed to him that he began to worship him. Let's look at Job's response to all the bad news as reported in Job 1:20–22 (AMP):

> Then Job got up and tore his robe and shaved his head [in mourning for the children], and he fell to the ground and worshiped [God]. He said, "Naked (without possessions) I came [into this world] from my mother's womb, and naked I will return there. The Lord gave and the Lord has taken away; blessed be the name of the Lord." Through all this Job did not sin nor did he blame God.

After all the difficulties and great loss he suffered, Job chose not to curse or badmouth God and die, like his wife had suggested. Job chose to keep his hope in God and to bless his name. He informed his wife that she should not speak and act so foolishly.

Then his wife said to him, "Do you still cling to your integrity [and your faith and trust in God, without blaming Him]? Curse God and die!" But he said to her, "You speak as one of the [spiritually] foolish women speaks [ignorant and oblivious to God's will]. Shall we indeed accept [only] good from God and not [also] accept adversity and disaster?" In [spite of] all this Job did not sin with [words from] his lips. (Job 2:9–10 AMP)

Even though He kills me; I will hope in Him. Nevertheless, I will argue my ways to His face. This also will be my salvation, for a godless man may not come before Him. (Job 13:15–16 AMP)

Instead, Job demonstrated before his wife that the presence of one's faith is not in the absence of doubt and unbelief. So in the face of difficulties, our prayers should be like in Mark 9:24 (AMP): "immediately the father of the boy cried out [with a desperate, piercing cry], saying, 'I do believe; help [me overcome] my unbelief.'"

The Three Friends of Job

Here comes Job's three friends: Eliphaz the Termanite, Bildad the Shuhite, and Zophar the Naamathite. They had heard about all of Job's troubles. They could not believe all that he was going through. He had not sinned in any way, but he still had all these troubles in his life. They went to sympathize and comfort him. When they saw him from a distance, they barely recognized him. The friends started weeping and tearing their clothes and sprinkling dust on their heads. All three tried to comfort and console him. However, Eliphaz, Bildad, and Zophar thought Job was hiding something from them, like an unconfessed sin that he needed to confess to God. Job's friends did not waver in their beliefs that Job's suffering was a result of sin. God would not have anyone to suffer innocently, so they advised him to repent and seek God's mercy and forgiveness.

Eliphaz, the first of Job's three friends, the chief, was a descendant of Teman. His name means "refined gold," but his fine gold was that of self-glory and being opinionated. As a wise man, he gloried in his own wisdom and represented the orthodox wisdom of his day. Eliphaz was a religious dogmatist. He told Job that all his afflictions—namely his sins—were judgments from God. Eliphaz stood firmly on his argument that Job was suffering because of his sin (Job 15:16). He then pointed out Job's path way to restoration (Job 22:21).

The Shuhite Bildad, son of debate, was another of Job's friends. He was known as the man who made a speech. Another meaning of Blidad's name is "Lord of Hadad," and "Hadad" means to shout. A strict dogmatist, Bildad was especially religious in human tradition. Bildad was known to be loud and animated in his declarations. He also pointed out that Job suffered because of his sin.

Zophar, the Naamathite, Job's third friend, prided himself on his knowledge of God. He was a religious dogmatist. Zophar, who assumed he knew all about God, thought he was a promoter of good living. He believed that if Job turned from his wrongdoing and hidden sin, God would restore him.

Job: A Man of Prayer and Worship

Not only did Job's wife misunderstand, misjudge, and spoke wrongly of him, his friends misunderstood him as he suffered. Although they stuck with him as he suffered, they were not sympathetic, encouraging, or comforting to Job through it all, the good, the bad, and the testing times. Job, a man of prayer, never stopped seeking and worshipping God through prayer. Job was like what Paul said in Philippians 4:12 (AMP): "I know how to get along and live humbly [in difficult times], and I also know how to enjoy abundance and live in prosperity. In any and every circumstance I have learned the secret [of facing life], whether well-fed or going hungry, whether having an abundance or being in need." Job knew how to have peace in and with God, even amid suffering. He never stopped praying. In the beginning of testing and trials, he prayed. And through the loss of it all, he prayed.

Finally at the end of his loss, testing, and suffering, Job did what he had always done, he prayed and worshipped God. Job did not become bitter; he did not retaliate or try to prove anything to anybody. He prayed, he worshipped, and he trusted and honored God till the end.

God, however, was not pleased with how Job three friends had treated him during his time of suffering. So they had to go to him and offer seven bullocks and seven rams as burnt offerings on their behalf. God then told them to go and have Job pray for them. These guys had to go humble themselves before the one person they accused of sinning and not repenting toward God. Job's three friends did as God instructed. Although his friends had treated him unjustly, Job, a mighty man of prayer, prayed for them as God had led him. And the Bible says that Job was restored with twice as much as before. Through it all, Job never stopped being committed to God as God was committed to him and continued to overwhelmingly honor, restore, and bless him.

> The Lord restored the fortunes of Job when he prayed for his friends, and the LORD gave Job twice as much as he had before. Then all his brothers and sisters and all who had known him before came to him, and they ate bread with him in his house; and they consoled him and comforted him over all the [distressing] adversities that the Lord had brought on him. And each one gave him a piece of money, and each a ring of gold. And the Lord blessed the latter days of Job more than his beginning; for he had 14,000 sheep, 6,000 camels, 1,000 yoke of oxen, and 1,000 female donkeys. (Job 42:10–12 AMP)

Chapter 9

KNOW HOW TO WAIT WITH ENDURANCE

Psalms 27; 40:1; 53:1, 118
Isaiah 26:340; 31
Proverbs 4:23, 7:1–3; 26:2
Hebrews 10:11, 38; 12:5
Romans 6:1–6; 7:14–25; 8:26–28; 12:8
2 Corinthians 5:17
James 1:1–8, 16–19
Colossians 3:16
Philippians 2:5–7; 3:12
Ephesians 4:22–24
Galatians 2:20
Timothy 6:6–12

Vernadette R. Augustusel

Keys on Waiting through Psalm 27 (AMP)

Persistent and Courageous Trust in God

Psalm 27:4
As you wait, consistently seek to dwell in God's presence:

> One thing I have asked of the Lord and that
> I will seek: That I may dwell in the house
> of the Lord [in His presence] all the days
> of my life, To gaze upon the beauty [the
> delightful loveliness and majestic grandeur]
> of the Lord And to meditate in His temple.

Psalm 27:5
As you wait, God will hide you in his secret place:

> For in the day of trouble He will hide me
> in His shelter; in the secret place of His
> tent He will hide me; He will lift me up
> on a rock.

Psalm 27:6
As you wait, offer up praise, thanksgiving, and worship unto
God the Father:

> And now my head will be lifted up above
> my enemies around me, in His tent I will
> offer sacrifices with shouts of joy; I will
> sing, yes, I will sing praises to the Lord.

Psalm 27:8
As you wait, pray and seek after God with all your heart:

> When you said, Seek my face [in prayer,
> require my presence as your greatest need],
> my heart said to you, your face, O Lord, I
> will seek [on the authority of your word].

Psalm 27:10
As you wait, know that all may leave and abandon you except for God; he won't, and he's always available for you:

> Although my father and my mother have
> abandoned me, yet the Lord will take me
> up [adopt me as his child].

Psalm 27:11
As you wait, know that God will teach, lead, and guide you out of a dark place, out of darkness on to a well-lighted path:

> Teach me your way, O Lord, and lead me
> on a level path because of my enemies [who
> lie in wait].

Psalm 27:13
As you wait, look for and expect to see the goodness of God.

> I would have despaired had I not believed
> that I would see the goodness of the Lord
> In the land of the living.

Psalm 27:14
As you wait, be fearless, confident, strong, and courageous, knowing that God is faithful and will answer you.

> Wait for and confidently expect the Lord;
> be strong and let your heart take courage;
> yes, wait for and confidently expect the Lord.

Arise in Victory

Worship always supersedes victory.

Sometimes while we are in the middle of being committed in a hard place, we will experience spiritual warfare. How we wait amid spiritual warfare is a huge part of our defense against the enemy and the outcome of our victory. When we engage in warfare, we sometimes have to be in the trenches. So just like natural armies and military people wait in the trenches, we must also wait in spiritual trenches before we move forward with our plan of attack. Our conduct in spiritual trenches is of vital importance. When we are in spiritual trenches, we don't have time to focus on foolishness, wasting our time on chaos and distractions from the right plan of attack. Galatians 5:22 (AMP) tells us, "But the fruit of the Spirit [the result of His presence within us] is love [unselfish concern for others] joy, [inner] peace, patience [not the ability to wait, but how we act while waiting], kindness, goodness, faithfulness."

While we are in the middle of challenges and waiting for things to turn around for us, we must learn and decide how to wait. How we wait is important, I believe, and it makes a big difference in whether we will be able to endure challenges throughout life and remain committed in a hard place. I believe a good outcome is contingent on how well we wait. God's Word reminds us to be confident in him while we wait in faith for things to change because waiting in faith pleases God. But my, "righteous one will live by faith. And I take no pleasure in the one who shrinks back (Hebrews 10:38). When we draw back in doubt, uncertainty, and unbelief, it does not please God. God the Father wants us to be patient while we wait on him—his plan, his provision, and his purpose for our lives. God said he knows the plans he have for us, good plans to give us hope and a future (Jeremiah 29:11). So it would make since to me that we should get to know God and wait on the Father, trusting and believing that we can't go wrong waiting on him. Isaiah 40:31 (AMP) says it this way: "But those who wait for the LORD [who expect, look for, and hope in Him] will gain new strength and renew their power; They will lift up their wings [and rise up close to God] like eagles [rising toward the sun]; they will run and not become weary, They will walk and not grow tired."

Friend, when we wait on God, looking to him and trusting his way, we will always have the strength to go on and be committed in a hard place. As we wait on God, we must not be consumed by our problems, troubles, and difficulties. We don't have to be consumed with the issues of life because we have helpers available to us—the Holy Spirit and the grace of God:

> I have been crucified with Christ [that is,
> in Him I have shared His crucifixion]; it
> is no longer I who live, but Christ lives in
> me. The life I now live in the body I live
> by faith [by adhering to, relying on, and
> completely trusting] in the Son of God,
> who loved me and gave Himself up for
> me. I do not ignore or nullify the [gracious
> gift of the] grace of God [His amazing,
> unmerited favor], for if righteousness comes
> through [observing] the Law, then Christ
> died needlessly. [His suffering and death
> would have had no purpose whatsoever].
> (Galatians 2:20–21 AMP)

When we wait with a good attitude, we will be able
to endure times of testing, trials, and difficulties. How we
wait is also a determining factor of if we will be able to be
committed in difficult times. Proverbs 4:23 tells us, "Above
all else, guard your heart, for everything you do flows from
it." We must be mindful of what is in our hearts while we
are waiting on God and for things to turn around in our
lives. Make sure bitterness is not resting in your bosom,
your heart. It is not good to harbor ill feelings in our hearts
toward anything or anyone. Being aware of where we are
spiritually is of most importance because we should not be
harsh, bitter, hardhearted, or hateful while we wait. People
become harsh and hateful when they are focused on their
difficulties, troubles, and problems rather than believing in
and trusting God for things to turn around for them. In
Hebrews 12:2 (AMP) it says,

[looking away from all that will distract us and] focusing our eyes on Jesus, who is the author and finisher of faith [the first incentive for our belief and the One who brings our faith to maturity], who for the joy [of accomplishing the goal] set before Him endured the cross disregarding the shame, and sat down at the right hand of the throne of God [revealing His deity, His authority, and the completion of His work].

While we are waiting, we should not be impatient or upset with God, others, or ourselves. Nor should we be worried or hopeless. We should be excited, knowing and trusting that God will come through on our behalf. Pray while you wait, hoping, trusting, and believing God. Be ready to seize the moments God told you about, and seize everything God promised. King David said that he would have fainted unless he had believed to see the goodness of God in the land of the living. In other words, if David was not looking to God, trusting him on every hand, he would have given up and thrown in the towel. Many of us feel like that from time to time, giving up when life come at us hard. Proverbs 3:5–6 reminds that we should, "Trust in the Lord with all your heart and lean not on your own understanding; in all your ways submit to him, and he will make your paths straight." Regardless of what happens, keep trusting and relying on the Lord. James 1:2–4 (AMP) put it this way:

> consider it nothing but joy, my brothers and sisters, whenever you fall into various trials. Be assured that the testing of your faith [through experience] produces endurance [leading to spiritual maturity, and inner peace]. And let endurance have its perfect result and do a thorough work, so that you may be perfect and completely developed [in your faith], lacking in nothing.

As people of God facing difficulties, we must still worship God. When we are looking to God and trusting him, we will forgive much, operate in kindness a little more, practice helpfulness where it is needed, be patient with those around us, and walk in the love of God a little more as we wait. King David was on to something when he realized the goodness of God being with him even when he did not get things right. King David said in Psalm 40:1–5 (AMP),

> I waited patiently and expectantly for the Lord; and He inclined to me and heard my cry. He brought me up out of a horrible pit [of tumult and of destruction], out of the miry clay, and He set my feet upon a rock, steadying my footsteps and establishing my path. He put a new song in my mouth, a song of praise to our God; many will see and fear [with great reverence] and will trust confidently in the Lord. Blessed [fortunate, prosperous, and favored by God] is the man who makes the Lord his trust, and does

not regard the proud or those who lapse into lies. Many, O Lord my God, are the wonderful works which you have done, and your thoughts toward us; there is none to compare with you. If I would declare and speak of your wonders, they would be too many to count.

Believe it or not, as the Word of God says, sometimes God disciplines those he loves, just like any loving parent who corrects his or her child to prevent harm to the child or others. God is also a loving parent who corrects his children. When we are going through the struggles of life, it is sometimes the result of our own doing or lifestyle. I'm convinced that we should want to line up with God and his Word, so we should question our lifestyles, actions, and reactions from time to time to see if we are living our best lives in the eyes of God. However, God is still faithful and just toward us, even during our struggles if they are of our own doing or otherwise. God patiently loves us through our troubles, problems, and difficulties, some of which we may have caused just to bring him glory. In these instances, it is my belief that God will not just leave us there in a state of defeat and hopelessness. Rather, God is faithful at all times. That is why we can wait patiently on the Lord God. God the Father is so awesome. Romans 8:28 states that "and we know that in all things God works for the good of those who love him, who have been called according to his purpose."

Stop Living Independently of God

The fool has says in his heart "there is no God." (Psalm 14:1)

Troubles and problems don't come into our lives without a cause. It has been said or believed that sometimes God allows trying times in our lives just to solve them and get the glory. Sometimes our troubles usher us to the place where God would have us to be, his perfect will.

> Now for a long time Israel was without the true God and without a teaching priest, and without [God's] law. but when they were in their trouble and distress they turned to the Lord God of Israel, and [in desperation earnestly] sought Him, and He let them find Him. In those times there was no peace for him who went out or for him who came in, for great suffering came on all the inhabitants of the lands. Nation was crushed by nation, and city by city, for God troubled them with every kind of distress. But as for you, be strong and do not lose courage, for there is reward for your work. (2 Chronicles 15:3–7 AMP)

Waiting with the Right Mindset

As we discussed in chapter 7 regarding the right mindset, I believe if we are going to be able to wait properly with a good attitude, we need to have the right mindset, the mind of Christ, a spiritual mindset. "And be continually renewed in the spirit of your mind [having a fresh, untarnished mental and spiritual attitude], and put on the new self [the regenerated and renewed nature], created in God's image, [godlike] in the righteousness and holiness of the truth [living in a way that expresses to God your gratitude for your salvation]" (Ephesians 4:23–24 AMP). When faced with trying times, it's easy to have a double mindset and not be sure what direction to go in when making decisions for a better life. We can't be faithful and fickle at the same time. So we must understand that no one can go or move in two directions at the same time in their emotions, mindsets, or even in their states of being. You can't complain and praise God at the same time. You can't be grateful for what you have and be unsatisfied with the life God has given you. You can't worry and worship and be thankful all at the same time. It is impossible to live a good life or enjoy life and be consumed by problems, troubles, and the worries of life. In Matthew 11:29, Jesus said that we should, "Take my yoke upon you and learn from me, for I am gentle and humble in heart, and you will find rest for your souls."

We also need the right mindset to wait on the Lord and be able to endure various challenges and hardships and remain committed in a hard place. Roman 12:2 reports, "Do not conform to the pattern of this world, but be transformed by the renewing of your mind. Then you will be able to test and approve what God's will is—his good, pleasing and perfect will."

If we allow the mind of Christ to be in us, we will be able to endure anything, regardless of what is happening with or around us. With the mind of Christ, you will be encouraged to endure in a hard place because Christ had the right mindset. Remember, Christ remained focused even in difficult times. You can even stay focused in a hard place, doing what you need to do with the right mindset so that you will not be consumed by life challenges and problems and can honestly say with confidences, "I'm redeemed."

Redeemed

> Therefore if anyone is in Christ [that is, grafted in, joined to Him by faith in Him as Savior], he is a new creature [reborn and renewed by the Holy Spirit]; the old things [the previous moral and spiritual condition] have passed away. Behold, new things have come [because spiritual awakening brings a new life]. (2 Corinthians 5:17 AMP)

Because we are redeemed people living in a fallen world, problems, confusion, and trouble will come. As redeemed people, we are responsible for taking active roles in spiritual growth and development as we allow God's Word to instruct and guide us in our daily lives. Redeemed people press on in faith and remain prayerful, no matter what the difficulty or challenge may be: "Day after day every priest stands and performs his religious duties; again and again he offers the same sacrifices, which can never take away sins" (Hebrews 10:11). God promises to care for his people and none of them will be lost: "The Lord redeems the soul of His servants, And none of those who take refuge in Him will be condemned (Psalm 34:22 AMP). Redeemed people don't do evil for evil.

Redeemed people understand and know that the issues of life flow out of their hearts, so they guard their hearts.

Redeemed people walk in the newness of life, understanding that they have to put away their old natures. Several scriptures help us with the redeemed mindset so that we can walk in our new natures.

> Regarding your previous way of life, you put off your old self [completely discard your former nature], which is being corrupted through deceitful desires, and be continually renewed in the spirit of your mind [having a fresh, untarnished mental and spiritual attitude],and put on the new self [the regenerated and renewed nature], created in God's image, [godlike] in the righteousness and holiness of the truth [living in a way that expresses to God your gratitude for your salvation]. (Proverbs 4:23 AMP)

> that, regarding your previous way of life, you put off your old self [completely discard your former nature], which is being corrupted through deceitful desires, and be continually renewed in the spirit of your mind [having a fresh, untarnished mental and spiritual attitude], and put on the new self [the regenerated and renewed nature], created in God's image, [godlike] in the righteousness and holiness of the truth

[living in a way that expresses to God your gratitude for your salvation]. (Ephesians 4:22–24 AMP)

Let the [spoken] word of Christ have its home within you [dwelling in your heart and mind—permeating every aspect of your being] as you teach [spiritual things] and admonish and train one another with all wisdom, singing psalms and hymns and spiritual songs with thankfulness in your hearts to God. (Colossians 3:16 AMP)

Mind Your Mouth

Let the words of my mouth and the meditation of my heart be acceptable and pleasing in Your sight, O Lord, my [firm, immovable] rock and my Redeemer. (Psalm 19:14 AMP)

Death and life are in the power of the tongue, and those who love it and indulge it will eat its fruit and bear the consequences of their words; (Proverbs 18:21 AMP).

Do everything without murmuring or questioning [the providence of God] (Philippians 2:14 AMP)

If you are not glorifying God and speaking positively, speaking encouraging words, encouraging others and self, then just be quiet. Believe it or not, what we say while we are going through and waiting for things to change while in a difficult place is important. We should stop talking negatively, just saying any and everything, especially during difficult times. If you can't say kind words of faith, just stop talking. Negative words, ill words that are spoken, I believe can create a negative atmosphere. And we know words have hurt people and destroyed lives. If you cannot speak words of faith while waiting and going through, just shut up because more than likely, you will make things worse. We need to be mindful of what is coming out of our mouths, My belief is that fussing, complaining, and just a using foul language can prolong your suffering, troubles, and deliverance, and even block your blessings. As God's people hoping for things to turn around for the better, we should be mindful of what we are saying particularly during hard times.

> Understand this, my beloved brothers and sisters; let everyone be quick to hear [be a careful, thoughtful listener], slow to speak [a speaker of carefully chosen words and], slow to anger [patient, reflective, forgiving]; for the [resentful, deep-seated] anger of man does not produce the righteousness of God [that standard of behavior which He requires from us]. So get rid of all uncleanness and all that remains of wickedness, and with a humble spirit receive the word [of God] which is implanted [actually rooted in your

heart], which is able to save your souls. But prove yourselves doers of the word [actively and continually obeying God's precepts], and not merely listeners [who hear the word but fail to internalize its meaning], deluding yourselves [by unsound reasoning contrary to the truth]. (James 1:19–22 AMP)

Chapter 10

PRAYERS AND INSTRUCTIONS FOR A REDEEMED LIFE

Dear friend, in order to possess the kingdom of God here on earth and be in covenant with God the Father, one must first come to know and understand who their heavenly Father is through a personal relationship with his Son, Jesus Christ. The only way one can have this relationship is by accepting Jesus Christ as your personal Lord and Savior. You can do this by first believing that Jesus Christ is Lord. Confess your sins and purposely turn from a lifestyle of sin, death, destruction, and damnation. You can surrender your life to God by praying this simple prayer and allowing him to fill your heart with His Holy Spirit.

> Father, in the name of Jesus, I recognize
> and acknowledge that I am a sinner. I now

repent and purposely turn from a life of sin, death, and destruction. I confess with my mouth and believe in my heart that Jesus Christ is Lord and that you raised him from the dead. I invite you, Lord Jesus, to come into my heart and into my life, and fill me with your Holy Spirit; guide and lead with your love. Thank you, Lord, for saving me. Amen.

Because if you acknowledge and confess with your mouth that Jesus is Lord [recognizing His power, authority, and majesty as God], and believe in your heart that God raised Him from the dead, you will be saved. For with the heart a person believes [in Christ as Savior] resulting in his justification [that is, being made righteous—being freed of the guilt of sin and made acceptable to God]; and with the mouth he acknowledges and confesses [his faith openly], resulting in and confirming [his] salvation. (Romans 10:9–10 AMP)

Welcome to the family of God according to Ephesians 2:19 (AMP): "So then you are no longer strangers and aliens [outsiders without rights of citizenship], but you are fellow citizens with the saints (God's people), and are [members] of God's household." Now that you have prayed and confessed Jesus as Lord and Savior, I pray that you will follow the simple instruction to develop a strong spiritual walk in life.

1. Pray, study, and obey God's Word daily. Be joyful and purposely walk in love (2 Timothy 3:16; 1 Thessalonians 5:16–18).
2. Find a good Bible-believing Church and join. Be faithful and committed in a local church. Don't let anything or anyone turn you back (Hebrews 10:25).
3. Get baptized by water (Matthew 3:6).
4. Pray and ask the Holy Spirit to baptize you in the Spirit with the evidence of speaking in tongues (Acts 2:3–4).
5. Remember that God's love will never fail you (John 3:16; 2 Corinthians 13:8).

If you fall in your daily walk with God, remember his love, get back up, and repent by purposely turning away from sin, and keep on walking with God.

In This Season, Stay Focused and Flexible

Worship will always shift the atmosphere in your favor. When we cry out in worship, our valley of dry bones comes alive. The enemy has to shut his mouth as we continuously walk in victory in any and every season of life. For when the enemy comes up against us to hinder and dismiss our gifts, talents, and opportunities, our worship will stop him in his tracks. Our worship will always be our road to breakthrough, breaking the back of the enemy. Troubles and problems may come to destroy us, but through our worship, we will witness abundant victory on a greater level. Please note that if we do not faint in our season of testing and difficulties, we will reap blessings due to a shift in the atmosphere because of our focus, flexibility, and worship.

Scripture References to Become Familiar With

2 Corinthians 4:8; 5:17–18; 10:5, 13
John 5:38–40; 14:1, 23–24
Mark 24:4
Romans 8:2
Hebrews 12:1–2; 13:5–6
Judges 10:13
James 1:2–18; 2:1, 22–25
Luke 4:8
Psalms 34:19; 42:5; 51:10; 55:22, 91; 138:8
Colossians 1:13, 27
Proverbs 5:18; 10:24
Philippians 4:4–8
Job 23:1
Jeremiah 29:11

Printed in the United States
By Bookmasters